## Table of Contents

**Faithful in Battle**

**Knights of Columbus Devotions for the Brave**

by

**Dr. ant**

Although the author and publisher have made every effort to ensure that the information in this book was correct at press time, the author and publisher do not assume and hereby disclaim any liability to any party for any loss, damage, or disruption caused by errors or omissions, whether such errors or omissions result from negligence, accident, or any other cause.

This publication is designed to provide accurate and authoritative information with regard to the subject matter covered. It is sold with the understanding that the publisher is not engaged in rendering professional services. If legal advice or other expert assistance is required, the services of a competent professional should be sought.

The fact that an organization or website is referred to in this work as a citation and/or a potential source of further information does not mean that the author or the publisher endorses the information the organization or website may provide or recommendations it may make.

Please remember that Internet websites listed in this work may have changed or disappeared between when this work was written and when it is read.

Faithful in Battle: Knights of Columbus Devotions for the Brave

**Contents**

## Appendix A: Appendix

### Prayers of the Saints

### Quotes from the Saints

### Historical Notes on the Knights of Columbus

## Introduction

The call to devotion and meditation is a profound invitation to every believer, forging a path towards deeper understanding and union with God. The purpose of this book is not merely to offer a collection of prayers and meditations, but to serve as a bridge that connects the faithful to the rich tradition of Roman Catholic spirituality. In these pages, we find a tapestry woven with the threads of the mysteries of the Rosary, the Franciscan Crown Rosary, the Seven Sorrows Servite Rosary, and the Divine Mercy Chaplet, all intertwined with reflections meant to elevate the soul and stir the heart.

Our journey begins with the intention to catechize the faithful and foster a robust understanding of their faith. The complexities of modern life often pull us in many directions, and it is easy for the soul to become weary. Yet, as St. Paul reminds us, "I can do all things through Christ which strengtheneth me" (Phil. 4:13). It is through meditative prayer and reflection that we draw strength, find clarity, and reclaim the peace that the world cannot give.

The Rosary, in particular, is a gift from the Blessed Mother that holds immense power. Each mystery is a step into the Gospel, inviting us to ponder the life of Christ with Mary as our guide. These mysteries are more than mere recollections; they are living moments that speak to our present circumstances, offering hope, comfort, and enlightenment.

The Joyful, Luminous, Sorrowful, and Glorious Mysteries of the Rosary each unfold unique aspects of Christ's life and mission. In contemplating these mysteries, we enter into a rhythm of grace that transforms our perspective and aligns our hearts with the divine. As St. Luke beautifully narrates the angel's announcement to Mary, "Hail, thou that art highly favoured, the Lord is with thee: blessed art thou among women" (Luke 1:28), we too are reminded of God's favor and presence in our lives.

Patriotism and devotion to one's country are also deeply embedded in the Catholic faith. This book seeks to inspire a love for one's homeland, seen through the lens of faith and guided by divine principles. For the Knights of Columbus, veterans, and patriots, the call to serve is a reflection of the highest form of charity—laying down one's life for others. Jesus Himself declared, "Greater love hath no man than this, that a man lay down his life for his friends" (John 15:13). In every act of service and sacrifice, we mirror Christ's ultimate act of love.

The Franciscan Crown Rosary presents yet another dimension of Marian devotion, focusing on the seven joys of Our Lady. These joys resonate with our own experiences of hope, renewal, and divine intervention. Reflecting on the Annunciation, Visitation, Nativity, and other joyful mysteries helps us to see God's work in our lives, even in the smallest details. As the angel said to Mary, "Fear not, Mary: for thou hast found favour with God" (Luke 1:30), we are reassured that God's favor rests upon us as well.

The Seven Sorrows Servite Rosary invites a meditative sorrow that purifies the soul and fortifies the heart. Reflecting on the prophecy of Simeon or the flight into Egypt brings us closer to understanding the depth of Mary's sorrow and her steadfast faith. These reflections help us to embrace our own sufferings with the same grace and fortitude, echoing Mary's resilience and trust in God's plan.

The Divine Mercy Chaplet, with its powerful prayers and meditations, calls us to place our trust entirely in

Jesus. In moments of weakness and doubt, we are reminded of His infinite mercy. "For with God nothing shall be impossible" (Luke 1:37). Trusting in Jesus, especially in the hour of mercy, illuminates the path to redemption and peace.

Throughout this book, the goal is to meld the rich traditions of the Catholic faith with practical applications for our daily lives. By delving deep into the mysteries, we not only enrich our spiritual lives but also become more effective witnesses to the truth of the Gospel. Evangelization begins in the heart—transformed and set ablaze by the love of Christ. It is our hope that these meditations will spark such a transformation.

The Eucharist, as the source and summit of our faith, remains central to these reflections. The profound mystery of Christ's body and blood, present under the appearances of bread and wine, beckons us into a divine communion that transcends time and space. As Jesus declared, "This is my body which is given for you: this do in remembrance of me" (Luke 22:19), we are called to a continual remembrance that shapes every aspect of our lives.

As priests, theologians, and philosophers have long pondered the truths of the faith, so too are we invited into this sacred contemplation. Each meditation offers an opportunity to encounter these truths afresh, with the hope that they will inspire deeper love and commitment to our Lord. The reflections and prayers in this book aim to be both a personal retreat and a communal celebration of faith.

In her apparitions, such as those at Fatima, Our Lady stresses the importance of the Rosary for peace and conversion. Her messages remain ever relevant, urging us towards penance, prayer, and the Eucharist. As we meditate on the mysteries, let us keep in mind her maternal guidance and intercession, trusting that she leads us ever closer to Jesus.

The unity of the Church, the Body of Christ, is also a fundamental theme. Each reflection not only strengthens personal devotion but also builds up the Church. Whether you are a Knight of Columbus serving the community, a veteran reflecting on sacrifices made, or a theologian seeking deeper understanding, this book aims to unite us in common purpose and shared faith. St. Paul's words ring true: "For as the body is one, and hath many members, and all the members of that one body, being many, are one body: so also is Christ" (1 Cor. 12:12).

Ultimately, this book is an invitation—to meditate, to pray, to serve, and to love. May you find these reflections a source of inspiration and strength, leading you to a closer walk with Christ and a more profound appreciation for the mysteries of our faith. In the words of our Savior, "Peace I leave with you, my peace I give unto you: not as the world giveth, give I unto you. Let not your heart be troubled, neither let it be afraid" (John 14:27). May His peace be with you always as you embark on this journey of devotion and discovery.

## Chapter 1: The Joyful Mysteries

Chapter 1 is a journey into the heart of divine joy, where the faithful are invited to unite their meditations with the blissful mysteries of Christ's early earthly life. From the moment the Angel Gabriel announced to Mary that she would bear the Son of God, "Behold, thou shalt conceive in thy womb, and bring forth a son, and shalt call his name Jesus" (Luke 1:31), to the sacred finding of the young Jesus astounding the teachers in the Temple, these events weave a tapestry of hope and divine purpose. The Joyful Mysteries stand as a testament to God's profound love for humanity, calling knights, patriots, and theologians alike to reflect upon these biblical truths with a heart full of praise and gratitude. As the faithful contemplate the Annunciation, Visitation, Nativity, Presentation, and the Finding of Jesus in the Temple, it becomes clear that each mystery unfolds a lesson in divine obedience, humility, and unwavering faith, urging us to follow the Virgin Mary's example and keep God's word alive in our hearts for the "kingdom of God is within you" (Luke 17:21).

## Reflections on the Annunciation

The Annunciation is an event that resonates deeply within the hearts of the faithful, embodying a pivotal moment in salvation history. When the Angel Gabriel appeared to Mary, it was not just a celestial encounter; it was the very moment when God's promise from the Old Testament began to take human form (Isaiah 7:14). In this encounter, the whispered prophecies reached their fruition in the fiat of a humble maiden, setting the stage for the incarnation of the divine.

The Annunciation invites us to reflect upon the virtue of humility. Mary, a young woman from Nazareth, was chosen to bear the Son of God. Her first reaction was natural and human: questioning, "How shall this be, seeing I know not a man?" (Luke 1:34). Yet, her ultimate response was imbued with profound faith and submission: "Behold the handmaid of the Lord; be it unto me according to thy word" (Luke 1:38). Her acceptance without hesitation demonstrates her unwavering trust in God's plan.

Mary's "yes" to God's will is a powerful testament to the beauty of obedience. In a culture that often celebrates autonomy, her submission is a countercultural act of faith. Obedience here is not blind or passive but an active and conscious embrace of divine will. As Christ would later echo in his life of perfect obedience to the Father, Mary's response at the Annunciation offers us a model of true discipleship. We are encouraged to ask ourselves: How often do we say "yes" to God's calling in our daily lives?

The role of the Angel Gabriel in the Annunciation also beckons us to consider the concept of divine messengers. Gabriel's greeting, "Hail, thou that art highly favoured, the Lord is with thee: blessed art thou among women" (Luke 1:28), affirms Mary's special place in divine providence. This angelic salutation, later embedded in the Hail Mary prayer, reminds us of the heavenly realm's active involvement in human affairs. Angels serve as God's emissaries, bringing hope, direction, and sometimes challenge, just as they did to Mary.

The Annunciation is intrinsically tied to the theme of incarnation—the Word made flesh. This mystery invites us to ponder the profound theological truth that in Jesus, divinity and humanity are perfectly united. John's Gospel poetically states, "And the Word was made flesh, and dwelt among us" (John 1:14). This union is not just a past event but an ongoing reality; Christ continues to dwell among us in the Eucharist, a point which later chapters will explore in greater detail.

Let us not overlook the role of the Holy Spirit in the Annunciation. Gabriel explains, "The Holy Ghost shall come upon thee, and the power of the Highest shall overshadow thee" (Luke 1:35). This overshadowing signifies divine action and presence, harking back to the Spirit hovering over the waters in the creation narrative (Genesis 1:2). The Holy Spirit's descent upon Mary signifies a new creation, a rebirth of humanity through Jesus Christ. Through reflection on this mystery, we can draw deeper into our relationship with the Holy Spirit, whose indwelling makes us children of God.

The moment Gabriel departed, Mary was left alone to ponder the magnitude of her calling. She was now bearing the Savior, yet her exterior life remained seemingly ordinary. This paradox of extraordinary grace amidst ordinary circumstances is a hallmark of Christian living. Often, God's most profound works are accomplished in the hidden corners of our everyday existence. Let us be reminded that our ordinary lives are fertile ground for divine encounters.

Reflecting on the Annunciation, we also acknowledge the element of divine timing. God's promise to send a savior, articulated through the prophets, came to fruition at a specific moment in history. Ecclesiastes reminds us, "To everything there is a season, and a time to every purpose under the heaven" (Eccles. 3:1). The Annunciation marks the onset of God's salvific plan unfolding in time. Our faith journey, too, operates within God's perfect timing, calling for patient trust in His providence.

The significance of Mary's virginity cannot be understated. As Gabriel announced, "The Holy Ghost shall come upon thee, and the power of the Highest shall overshadow thee: therefore also that holy thing which shall be born of thee shall be called the Son of God" (Luke 1:35). Her virgin motherhood points to the unique, miraculous nature of Jesus's birth. This purity is both a sign of Mary's total consecration to God and a fulfillment of Isaiah's prophecy about a virgin bearing a son (Isaiah 7:14). It calls us to a purity of heart, to be wholly dedicated to God's work.

Indeed, Mary's pivotal role in the Annunciation embodies the cooperation between divine grace and human freedom. She was chosen by God yet retained full freedom in her response. This interplay highlights a core tenet of our faith: while God initiates, He always respects human freedom. Our salvation history is a testament to God's invitation and humanity's response. Mary's cooperation with grace calls us to recognize the importance of our own free will in responding to God's invitations.

Furthermore, when we reflect on the Annunciation, we must not overlook the joy inherent in this event. The news brought by Gabriel is the beginning of the "Good News" for all humanity. The anticipation of Christ's arrival is a cause for deep, abiding joy, a theme that resonates through Mary's Magnificat: "My soul doth magnify the Lord, And my spirit hath rejoiced in God my Saviour" (Luke 1:46-47). This joy is rooted in the fulfillment of God's promises, a joy available to us as we live in the light of Christ's coming.

In contemplating the Annunciation, we are called to emulate Mary's virtues. Her humility, obedience, faith, and joy are not just admirable traits but are pathways to deepen our union with God. Each Hail Mary we recite as part of the Rosary is an opportunity to reflect on these virtues and to seek Mary's intercession in embodying them in our own lives. The Annunciation is a call to surrender our lives to God's will with the same trust and openness that Mary displayed.

As we meditate on this profound mystery, let us also be mindful of the broader implications it holds for the Christian community. Mary's fiat was an individual act that had communal ramifications, bringing forth the salvation of the world. Our personal acts of faith and obedience likewise contribute to the spiritual welfare of the Church. Through the Annunciation, we are reminded that our small "yes" to God can have far-reaching effects, weaving into the larger tapestry of God's redemptive work.

The Annunciation calls us to a renewed awareness of the sacred in the ordinary, urging us to live our lives with the expectation that God can and does intervene in our world. It encourages us to be attentive to the whispers of the Holy Spirit, ready to respond with courage and faith. In reflecting on Mary's encounter with Gabriel

## Meditations on the Visitation

As we dive into the second Joyful Mystery, the Visitation offers us a tapestry of humility, joy, and divine providence. This event, described in the Gospel of Luke, reveals deep spiritual truths that resonate with our lives even today (Luke 1:39-56). It begins with Mary's immediate response to the news from the angel Gabriel, not only about her own role as the Mother of God but also about her relative Elizabeth's miraculous pregnancy. Without hesitation, Mary undertakes the journey to the hill country of Judah to visit Elizabeth. This act of selflessness and charity reflects the profound love and solidarity that should characterize our own Christian walk.

Mary's visit is not a mere social call; it is a meeting rich with theological significance. When Elizabeth hears Mary's greeting, the infant leaping in her womb is a divine acknowledgment of the Messiah's presence. Elizabeth, filled with the Holy Ghost, exclaims, "Blessed art thou among women, and blessed is the fruit of thy womb" (Luke 1:42). These words echo through time, continually reminding us of the special role that Mary plays in the plan of salvation.

This mystery encapsulates the essence of divine joy and human humility. Despite her immense role in God's plan, Mary remains the epitome of humility. She does not boast of her unique position but instead shares in Elizabeth's joy and serves her through the visitation. The deep connection between Mary and Elizabeth is a testament to the beauty of human relationships founded on faith and divine grace. Their interaction demonstrates an unparalleled bond that goes beyond mere kinship, revealing the unity and love that flows from those who trust in God's providence.

Mary's Magnificat, her song of praise, is a brilliant exposition of biblical themes. "My soul doth magnify the Lord, And my spirit hath rejoiced in God my Saviour" (Luke 1:46-47). Here, Mary highlights the core Christian attitude—humble recognition of God's greatness and boundless mercy. She acknowledges God as her Savior, reflecting her profound humility and gratitude, even as she carries the Savior of the world. This prayer serves as a poignant reminder for each of us to maintain an attitude of thanksgiving, regardless of our circumstances.

The Visitation also invites us to consider the virtue of hope. Elizabeth and Zechariah had longed for a child for many years, and the visit from Mary signifies the fulfillment of divine promises. Their story mirrors our own moments of waiting and longing for God's intervention in our lives. When Mary arrives, carrying the unborn Jesus, she brings not just the promise of new life but the hope of redemption. This reminds us that every visit, every encounter in our lives, holds the potential for God's grace to break through.

In this mystery, we see the Holy Spirit at work, inspiring Elizabeth to recognize and proclaim Mary's blessedness. This divine inspiration serves as a reminder that the Holy Spirit is always present and active in our lives, guiding us to recognize God's work around us. The acknowledgment of Jesus' presence within Mary by Elizabeth prompts us to acknowledge and recognize Christ in our lives and the lives of others.

The journey of Mary to visit Elizabeth also teaches us about the importance of service and sacrifice. Mary's decision to travel a great distance to help her elderly relative, despite her own extraordinary situation, underscores the Christian call to serve others. We are reminded of Jesus' words, "For even the Son of man came not to be ministered unto, but to minister, and to give his life a ransom for many" (Mark 10:45). Mary's actions prefigure this ultimate act of service.

As Catholics, meditating on the Visitation fosters a deep sense of community and solidarity. The meeting between Mary and Elizabeth is a powerful example of how God works through relationships to fulfill His divine plan. Elizabeth's joyful reception of Mary, and the prophetic leap of John the Baptist in her womb, reaffirms the sanctity of life at all stages. Their encounter also prompts us to celebrate and support the family as a fundamental unit where faith and love flourish.

The joyous interchange between Mary and Elizabeth prompts introspection about how we greet and support one another. Do we, like Elizabeth, recognize and affirm the presence of God in others? Do we, like Mary, bring Christ into our interactions, serving others with love and humility? Reflecting on the Visitation encourages us to foster a spirit of mutual encouragement and recognition of God's work in our community.

Moreover, the Visitation beckons us to trust in God's timing. Elizabeth's pregnancy, like Mary's, came at an unexpected time, demonstrating God's power to fulfill

His promises in surprising ways. Our own lives are filled with moments where divine timing differs from our own expectations. This mystery teaches us to remain patient and faithful, trusting that God's plans for us are perfect and will unfold in due time.

On a deeper level, the Visitation can be seen as a microcosm of the Church's mission – to bring Christ to others joyfully and to be the presence of Christ in a world often longing for hope and redemption. Mary's visit to Elizabeth is an act of evangelization, carrying the Good News to her relative. We are called to follow her example by bringing Christ into our everyday encounters, witnessing to His love and truth.

In our spiritual lives, regularly meditating on the Visitation can help us grow in virtues like charity, humility, and gratitude. It prompts us to take action, serving others selflessly just as Mary did, and to celebrate the joy of others, magnifying the Lord together. As we reflect on this mystery, we should ask the Blessed Mother to accompany us in our journey of faith, helping us to recognize and respond to God's presence in our lives and the lives of others with joy and love.

In conclusion, the Visitation is much more than a historical event; it's a living lesson in divine joy, humility, and service. Through this meditation, we are called to deepen our understanding of God's love and our role in His divine plan. Let us, inspired by Mary's example, strive to be bearers of Christ's love and grace, continually seeking to serve and uplift one another.

## Contemplations on the Nativity

The Nativity of our Lord Jesus Christ marks a pivotal moment in human history. The infinite God humbled Himself and took on human flesh, entering our world in the humblest of circumstances. This mystery, celebrated by Roman Catholics, is a testament to God's profound love for mankind, a love that is difficult to fathom yet deeply reassuring.

Consider the scene: Mary and Joseph in a stable because there was no room for them in the inn. This humble setting was where the King of Kings chose to be born. The world, busy and preoccupied, did not recognize the momentous event unfolding in Bethlehem. Reflect on the simplicity of the Nativity scene and the profound lessons it offers in humility and the rejection of worldly pride.

"And so it was, that, while they were there, the days were accomplished that she should be delivered. And she brought forth her firstborn son, and wrapped him in swaddling clothes, and laid him in a manger; because there was no room for them in the inn" (Luke 2:6-7). This passage evokes a wealth of emotions and spiritual reflections. The swaddling clothes symbolize the human vulnerability that Christ willingly embraced. The manger, often depicted as a feeding trough, foreshadows the Eucharist where Christ feeds the faithful with His own body and blood.

In contemplating the Nativity, one cannot ignore the shepherds, who were the first to receive the heavenly announcement of Christ's birth. The angel's words, "For unto you is born this day in the city of David a Saviour, which is Christ the Lord" (Luke 2:11), resonate through the ages. The shepherds, representing the humble and the meek, teach us about the importance of being open to divine messages and the joy that comes from encountering Christ.

The shepherds' immediate response upon hearing the angelic proclamation serves as a model for us: "And they came with haste, and found Mary, and Joseph, and the babe lying in a manger" (Luke 2:16). Their urgency and joy in seeking the Christ Child challenge us to respond with similar enthusiasm and fervor in our own faith journeys. Are we as eager to seek out and recognize Christ in our daily lives?

Moving from the shepherds to the Magi, we see a different group of individuals drawn to Christ. The Wise

Men from the East saw His star and embarked on a long journey to pay homage. Their story highlights the universal call to salvation; Christ came for all humanity, breaking down barriers of race, nationality, and status. As the Magi laid their gifts of gold, frankincense, and myrrh at the feet of Jesus, we are reminded of the need to offer the best of ourselves to God.

The Magi's journey also calls attention to the search for truth and the willingness to go great lengths to find it. They did not allow distance, discomfort, or danger to hinder their quest. "When they saw the star, they rejoiced with exceeding great joy" (Matt. 2:10). Their joy was complete upon encountering Christ, teaching us that our own joy is found in drawing near to Him.

Mary, the Mother of Jesus, offers yet another dimension of contemplation. She, who said "Behold the handmaid of the Lord; be it unto me according to thy word" (Luke 1:38), held the divine infant in her arms. Her fiat, her yes to God, allowed the Incarnation to happen. In reflecting on Mary's role in the Nativity, we are invited to ponder on our own willingness to say yes to God's will and to be instruments of His grace.

As we meditate on this scene, we witness a convergence of humility, royalty, and divine providence. Everything about the Nativity invites us to a deeper theological understanding and a more heartfelt spiritual experience. The cattle lowing, the angels singing, and the silence of the night all combine to create an atmosphere of sacred wonder.

Joseph, the silent guardian of the Holy Family, is another figure worthy of deep reflection. His obedience and protection of Mary and Jesus are models of faithful fatherhood and steadfast devotion. Joseph's silent strength points us to the importance of quiet yet firm dedication to God's will. His role in the Nativity challenges us to be protective and nurturing in our own vocations, whatever they may be.

The Nativity also reflects the fulfillment of ancient prophecies, such as those found in Isaiah: "For unto us a child is born, unto us a son is given: and the government shall be upon his shoulder: and his name shall be called Wonderful, Counsellor, The mighty God, The everlasting Father, The Prince of Peace" (Isa. 9:6). The birth of Christ is not an isolated event but a culmination of centuries of divine promises and preparation.

Each detail of the Nativity, from the star over Bethlehem to the swaddling clothes, is imbued with rich symbolism. The star symbolizes divine guidance and illumination, leading the Magi to the Savior. It beckons us to follow the light of Christ, the light that dispels darkness and brings hope to the world. The swaddling clothes, reminiscent of burial cloths, subtly hint at the sacrifice Christ would later make for humanity's redemption.

The angels' proclamation of "Glory to God in the highest, and on earth peace, good will toward men" (Luke 2:14) is a timeless message that calls us to glory in God's majesty and to strive for peace and goodwill among ourselves. The birth of Christ is a call to reflect God's love in our interactions with others, fostering harmony and unity.

Reflecting on the Nativity within the context of the Joyful Mysteries, we understand it as not only an event of historical significance but also a source of ongoing spiritual nourishment. The Nativity, as a mystery of joy, invites us to enter into a deeper relationship with Christ, to welcome Him into our hearts as eagerly as the shepherds and the Magi welcomed Him into the world.

In conclusion, the Nativity of our Lord Jesus Christ is a profound mystery that calls for deep contemplation and reflection. It is a celebration of divine love, humility, and the fulfillment of God's promises. As we meditate on this sacred event, may we be inspired to cultivate a spirit of humility, to seek Christ with fervor, and to offer our lives as gifts to God. Let the Nativity remind us of our own call to reflect God's love and truth in the world, bringing His peace and goodwill to all we encounter.

## Insights on the Presentation in the Temple

The Presentation in the Temple holds a profound place in the hearts of the faithful, illuminating the essence of devotion, obedience, and divine prophecy. As we meditate on this joyful mystery, we are invited to step into the scene in Jerusalem, where Joseph and Mary, in humble conformity with Jewish law, bring their firstborn Son to present Him to the Lord. This act not only adhered to the Law of Moses but also revealed Jesus as the fulfillment of that very law. "As it is written in the law of the Lord, Every male that openeth the womb shall be called holy to the Lord" (Luke 2:23).

In offering Jesus to God, Mary and Joseph exemplify the virtue of obedience, a cornerstone of our faith. Their willingness to follow God's command, despite the extraordinary circumstances of Jesus' divine conception and birth, teaches us the importance of adhering to God's will in our own lives. Through their example, we learn to surrender our desires and plans to embrace God's greater plan for us. This surrender comes with a promise—that God's plan, though sometimes mysterious and challenging, leads us to our true purpose and ultimate joy.

As they enter the temple, the Holy Family encounters Simeon, a devout man "waiting for the consolation of Israel" (Luke 2:25). The Holy Spirit had revealed to Simeon that he would not see death before he had seen the Messiah. Simeon's canticle, known as the Nunc Dimittis, is a profound expression of fulfilled hope: "Lord, now lettest thou thy servant depart in peace, according to thy word: For mine eyes have seen thy salvation" (Luke 2:29-30). His encounter with Jesus manifests the longing of the human heart for divine communion, a longing that is fulfilled in Christ.

This moment in the temple is not just a meeting of individuals; it is a convergence of prophecies and promises, centuries in the making. The presentation signifies the fulfillment of God's covenant with Israel and the advent of a new era in salvation history. The light of revelation that Simeon speaks of is not just for Israel but for "the Gentiles" as well, highlighting the universality of Jesus' mission (Luke 2:32).

Simultaneously, the Prophetess Anna, a symbol of perseverance and faith, gives thanks to God and speaks of the child to all who were looking forward to the redemption of Jerusalem. Her life, devoted to fasting and prayer, culminates in the joy of witnessing the

Messiah. Anna's actions encourage us to remain steadfast in our faith practices, trusting that our devotion will lead us to divine encounters.

The prophecy of Simeon also casts a shadow on this joyful scene. He foretells that Jesus is "set for the fall and rising again of many in Israel; and for a sign which shall be spoken against; (Yea, a sword shall pierce through thy own soul also)" (Luke 2:34-35). These words, directed at Mary, allude to the suffering she will endure as she witnesses her Son's Passion. This prophetic insight reminds us that joy and sorrow often intertwine in our journey of faith. It is through Mary's pierced heart that we learn the depth of her participation in God's salvific plan.

The Presentation in the Temple has significant spiritual implications for the Knights of Columbus, Patriots, and Veterans. The virtues of obedience, sacrifice, and prophetic vision present in this mystery resonate deeply with the ethos of service and dedication to the greater good. Just as Mary and Joseph presented Jesus, those in service are called to present their lives as living sacrifices, committed to the enduring values of faith and duty. In contemplating this mystery, the faithful are inspired to renew their own commitments to God, country, and community.

For priests and theologians, this mystery invites a deeper reflection on the interplay between law and grace. The adherence to Mosaic Law by the Holy Family, coupled with the prophecies spoken in the temple, bridges the Old and New Covenants. It is a testament to the continuity of God's salvific plan and the unfolding mystery of the Incarnation. The Presentation underscores the importance of liturgical rites and ceremonies in revealing and participating in divine truths.

Philosophers might find a wealth of contemplation in the themes of fulfillment and prophetic witness that emerge in this narrative. The presentation is both an end and a beginning—a fulfillment of the Law and the prophecy, and the inauguration of Jesus' public manifestation. It invites philosophical inquiry into the nature of time, history, and divine revelation.

Moreover, this mystery reminds us of the communal nature of faith. The temple, a place of worship and community, becomes the backdrop for this divine encounter. The presence of Simeon and Anna highlights the role of the faith community in recognizing and affirming God's work in the world. It is within the context of community that we encounter God most profoundly, supporting and upholding one another in our spiritual journeys.

As we continue to meditate on the Presentation in the Temple, let us immerse ourselves in the joy and prophetic hope that this mystery embodies. Let us seek to emulate the faith and obedience of Mary and Joseph, the hope and witness of Simeon, and the perseverance and proclamation of Anna. May this contemplation deepen our understanding of God's salvific work and inspire us to present our own lives as offerings to His divine will.

In conclusion, the Presentation in the Temple is a profound tapestry of faith, obedience, prophecy, and community. It calls us to reflect on our own lives, to recognize the divine in the everyday, and to commit ourselves to God's greater plan with joyful hearts. Let us carry this mystery with us, allowing it to illuminate our paths and strengthen our faith as we journey closer to God, ever inspired by the Holy Family's example.

## Thoughts on the Finding of Jesus in the Temple

The Fifth Joyful Mystery, the Finding of Jesus in the Temple, portrays a profound moment not only in the Holy Family's lives but also in the life of every believer. This event, depicted in Luke's Gospel, is loaded with spiritual significance and resonates with the experiences of loss and discovery that are common to humanity. Mary and Joseph's anxious search leads to a deeply relational revelation that Jesus is always in His Father's house, guiding hearts towards the truth.

After three days of frantic searching, Mary and Joseph found Jesus in the Temple, sitting among the teachers, listening to them, and asking questions. Their relief is palpably human, an echo of every parent's worry and subsequent joy upon finding a lost child. But in this divine encounter, there's an added layer of profound theological insight. Jesus' response to His Mother, "How is it that ye sought me? wist ye not that I must be about my Father's business?" (Luke 2:49), establishes His divine mission, early in His earthly life, as one inexorably linked to the Father's will.

Mary and Joseph's experience invites us to reflect on our own spiritual journeys. Their search symbolizes the moments of darkness and uncertainty we all face. Yet, this mystery reassures us that Christ is never truly lost; He waits for us in the sacred spaces of our lives, often where we least expect to find Him. The Temple represents the Church, our community of faith, where Jesus continues to dwell, offering wisdom and solace.

This episode also signifies a pivotal moment for Christ's followers, highlighting the importance of prioritizing our relationship with God amidst the hustle of daily life. Mary and Joseph's relentless search for Jesus is an exemplar of faith, one that calls upon every believer to seek Christ ardently, especially in challenging times. Their unwavering determination to find Him should inspire a relentless pursuit of holiness and understanding.

Moreover, this mystery speaks to the role of young Jesus as a teacher. In the Temple, He astounded the learned scholars with His wisdom and understanding, an indication of the infinite wisdom of God made manifest in the child Jesus. Here, we see a foreshadowing of His later public ministry, where He would teach with authority and grace, urging people toward conversion and deeper faith. It is in this setting that we witness the harmonious blend of His divine nature and human upbringing.

Simeon's prophecy at the Presentation in the Temple finds a minor fulfillment here. "A light to lighten the Gentiles, and the glory of thy people Israel" (Luke 2:32). Jesus, even as a youth, shines as a beacon of knowledge and truth in a place of learning and worship, illustrating that He is indeed that light prophesied.

The Finding of Jesus in the Temple also poignantly highlights the sorrows that would punctuate the lives of Mary and Joseph. Their profound anxiety during the search anticipates the future suffering they would endure, especially Mary, who would one day see her Son crucified. This event provides a microcosm of their forthcoming trials, reminding us that even in times of agony, faith guides the way to eventual joy and reunion.

Contemplating this mystery encourages deeper devotion to the Holy Family. It's an invitation to see in Mary and Joseph, models of fervent parental love, fidelity, and patience. Their relationship with Jesus reminds us of the sanctity found in family life and the importance of nurturing faith within the household, teaching that even amidst confusion and heartache, divine guidance is always present.

As we meditate on this mystery, we are called to humility. Jesus, though divine, submits Himself to earthly parents in a humble family setting. He respects and obeys them, underscoring the virtues of obedience and respect that all faithful are called to embody. This submission is a testament to the profound mystery of the Incarnation, where the Word made flesh abides by human limitations to redeem humanity.

Let us also not overlook the silence of Joseph in scripture, often unnoticed but powerful. His quiet strength and action speak louder than words, demonstrating a profound trust in God's plan. His role serves as a reminder of the silent, faithful workers in the vineyard of the Lord, reflecting the quiet power of steadfast faith and action.

Furthermore, the Temple encounter reflects the significance of religious tradition and the role it plays in nurturing faith. The Passover festival brought the Holy Family to Jerusalem, and it was during this religious observance that Jesus stayed behind, immersing Himself in discussions about His Father's business.

This deeply ingrained tradition provided the backdrop for Jesus' first recorded words. It emphasizes the role of sacred rituals in leading us to deeper encounters with God.

In praying the Fifth Joyful Mystery, we not only commemorate an event in Jesus' life but also invite reflections on our own spiritual practices. Are we seeking Christ in our daily lives? Are we open to finding Him in our places of worship, community events, or even in unexpected conversations? This mystery calls us to be vigilant, to trust in God's timing, and to have faith that, like Mary and Joseph, we will find Jesus guiding us to His Father's house.

Finally, this mystery invites a broader reflection on our own lives as pilgrims. The Holy Family's annual journey to Jerusalem symbolizes our own spiritual pilgrimages. Each of us is on a journey toward a deeper union with God, sometimes filled with detours and moments of searching. Yet, in our persistent and faithful search, we are promised the joy of finding Christ anew, ready to illuminate our path with His wisdom and love. To seek and to find Jesus in the "temple" of our hearts and communities should be the ultimate goal that brings perennial joy to our spiritual journey.

## Chapter 2: The Luminous Mysteries

The Luminous Mysteries, also known as the Mysteries of Light, usher us into Christ's public ministry, radiating divine grace and illuminating the truth of the Gospel. As we meditate on these bright moments, let us be moved by the deep waters of Jesus' Baptism in the Jordan, where the heavens opened and the Spirit descended like a dove, proclaiming, "Thou art my beloved Son; in thee I am well pleased" (Mark 1:11). We then witness the first miracle at the Wedding of Cana, a testament to Mary's intercession and Christ's divine authority to transform, symbolized by turning water into wine. Progressing through these sacred histories, we encounter Jesus' proclamation of the Kingdom of God, which calls us to repentance and faith. At the Transfiguration, His divine glory is revealed to Peter, James, and John, affirming the fulfillment of the Law and the Prophets as He stands between Moses and Elijah. Finally, in the Institution of the Eucharist, Christ offers His body and blood, a new covenant and eternal sacrifice, encapsulating the very heart of our redemption. In these mysteries, let us find motivation to deepen our faith, unwavering hope, and selfless love, ever praising God for His infinite mercy and grace.

## Reflections on the Baptism of Jesus in the Jordan

The Baptism of Jesus in the Jordan by John the Baptist marks the beginning of Christ's public ministry and stands as a profound mystery rich in meaning and significance. In this luminous event, we see the confluence of divinity and humanity, affirming Jesus' divine sonship while underscoring His solidarity with us sinners. As we meditate on this mystery, let us immerse ourselves in the waters of Jordan, pondering the depths of God's love and the call to repentance and new life.

The Gospel according to Saint Matthew provides a moving account of this momentous event: "And Jesus, when he was baptized, went up straightway out of the water: and, lo, the heavens were opened unto him, and he saw the Spirit of God descending like a dove, and lighting upon him: And lo a voice from heaven, saying, This is my beloved Son, in whom I am well pleased" (Matt. 3:16-17). This divine affirmation echoes through the ages, affirming not only Jesus' identity but also the Trinitarian mystery revealed in the Father's voice, the Son present in the waters, and the Spirit descending like a dove.

In the act of baptism, Jesus sanctifies the waters and prefigures our own baptism, where we are cleansed from sin and reborn as children of God. It is an invitation to contemplate the grace and transformative power of this sacrament. As St. John of the Cross teaches, the trials and purifications we undergo are purposed to draw us closer to Divine Love. Indeed, in reflecting on the Baptism of Christ, we are called to renew our own baptismal promises and commitments.

Imagine John the Baptist at the Jordan River, clothed in camel's hair, embodying the prophetic tradition. John's mission was clear: to prepare the way for the Lord by calling people to repentance. He proclaimed, "I indeed baptize you with water unto repentance: but he that cometh after me is mightier than I, whose shoes I am not worthy to bear: he shall baptize you with the Holy Ghost, and with fire" (Matt. 3:11). Even John, the greatest among those born of women, perceived the greatness and holiness of Jesus.

John's humility before Christ sets an example for us. In our pursuit of faith and devotion, humility must serve as our cornerstone. Knights of Columbus, veterans, and all who seek to embody virtues of courage and service must also anchor their strength in the humility of

Christ, who came not to be served, but to serve. This humility is not weakness but a profound strength born of love and self-giving.

Reflecting on the baptism further guides us to think about our mission as Christians in the world. Jesus' baptism marked the beginning of His mission to proclaim the Kingdom of God. From that moment, His message was one of repentance, healing, and liberation. Similarly, we are called to be ambassadors of Christ, bearing witness to the transformative power of God's love in our families, communities, and the world.

Although Jesus was sinless, His willingness to undergo baptism was an act of profound humility and solidarity. By entering the waters of the Jordan, He identified with humanity's brokenness and took upon Himself our sins, foreshadowing His ultimate sacrifice on the cross. His baptism is a sign of His commitment to walk the path of suffering and redemption. In our own lives, embracing our crosses with faith and hope becomes a participation in the redemptive mission of Jesus.

In considering the symbolism of water in Scripture, we find a richness that deepens our understanding of baptism. Water signifies both death and life; it has the power to destroy as in the flood during Noah's time, but it also has the power to sustain and give life. At the baptismal font, the waters become for us a source of new life, washing away the old self and bestowing the gift of the Holy Spirit. As St. Paul writes, "Therefore we are buried with him by baptism into death: that like as Christ was raised up from the dead by the glory of the Father, even so we also should walk in newness of life" (Rom. 6:4).

This newness of life calls us to a radical conversion and commitment to live out the fruits of baptism. It is no longer we who live, but Christ who lives in us, guiding our actions, words, and decisions. Our daily lives, then, become a reflection of this transformative grace, challenging us to combat the evils of the world with the goodness and mercy of the Gospel.

Moreover, the Baptism of Jesus is a powerful reminder of the communal nature of our faith. While it is deeply personal, baptism incorporates us into the Body of Christ, the Church. This communal aspect underscores our responsibility to support and uphold one another in our spiritual journeys. As members of the Church, we share in its mission to teach, govern, and sanctify, encouraging each other to grow in faith, hope, and charity.

Let us take inspiration from the saints and martyrs who lived their baptismal promises with unwavering faith. Their lives are testaments to the enduring power of God's grace at work in the world. From St. Peter, whose bold proclamation at Pentecost drew multitudes to baptism, to modern-day saints who lived and died for Christ, we find examples of courage, conviction, and holiness.

In our moments of doubt and struggle, let us turn to the moment of Christ's baptism for strength and reassurance. The heavens were opened, and the voice of the Father resounded. This same assurance is extended to each of us: we are beloved children of God, called to live in His grace and truth. Whether we are theologians contemplating the mysteries of faith or laypeople striving to live out our baptismal call in daily life, the Baptism of Jesus remains a wellspring of inspiration and strength.

In conclusion, the Baptism of Jesus in the Jordan is a luminous mystery that draws us into a deeper understanding of our faith and calling. It challenges us to embrace humility, renew our commitment to God, and participate in the redeeming work of Christ. As we meditate on this mystery, let us allow the Spirit to guide us, transforming our hearts and minds to reflect the light of Christ in a world in need of His love and mercy.

May our reflections on this sacred event deepen our devotion and lead us to a more profound relationship with the Holy Trinity, affirming our identity as children of God and our mission to make His love known to all.

**meditations on the wedding at cana**

The miracle at the Wedding at Cana marks the beginning of Jesus' public ministry. This first of His signs not only reveals His divine power but also underscores His compassionate understanding of human needs. It is at this humble wedding feast that our Lord chooses to perform His initial miracle, turning water into wine, thereby shedding light on a deeper spiritual reality.

In reflecting on the Wedding at Cana, we are reminded of the words of John, "And both Jesus was called, and his disciples, to the marriage" (John 2:2). The very presence of Jesus and His disciples signifies the importance of marriage in the Christian life. At the heart of this celebration is the union of a man and a woman, a sacramental covenant that mirrors Christ's relationship with His Church. This synergy affirms the sanctity of marriage and calls us to honor our own vocational commitments.

Mary's role at the Wedding at Cana cannot be overstated. She perceives the need even before others do, gently bringing it to her Son's attention: "They have no wine" (John 2:3). Her maternal intercession exemplifies the way she continues to intercede for us from heaven, bringing our petitions to her Son with compassionate urgency. "Whatsoever he saith unto you, do it" (John 2:5), instructs Mary. Here, she offers her last recorded words in the Bible, encapsulating her enduring wisdom and trust in Jesus' divine will.

The six stone water jars were filled to the brim upon Jesus' command. This meticulous detail highlights the abundance of God's grace—overflowing, inexhaustible, and accessible to all who seek it. When Jesus transforms the water into wine, it symbolizes the new covenant brought about through His ministry, offering spiritual rejuvenation and celebration of God's unending love.

Moreover, the miracle of Cana also illuminates how Jesus implicitly honors His mother. His initial response to Mary, "Woman, what have I to do with thee? mine hour is not yet come" (John 2:4), seems distant. Yet, His subsequent actions strengthen our understanding that the timing of His public works indeed acknowledges Mary's advocacy. It paints a vivid portrait of obedience and respect within the Holy Family, one that invites us to re-examine our own familial relationships through the same divine lens.

Let us consider the significance of the wine itself. Wine, often associated with joy and celebration, signifies the superabundant spiritual blessings that Christ brings to our lives. The headwaiter's reaction to the new wine—"Every man at the beginning doth set forth good wine; and when men have well drunk, then that which is worse: but thou hast kept the good wine until now" (John 2:10)— can be seen as a metaphor for how God's gifts often come when least expected, surpassing our human anticipations and elevating our earthly experiences to foretaste the heavenly banquet.

As Knights of Columbus, priests, theologians, and patriots, the Wedding at Cana calls us to reflect on our mission to serve others in need. Our Lord's miracle was performed out of compassion and a desire to preserve the joy of the celebration. This act challenges us to be instruments of God's grace, promoting the sanctity of marriage and family whether in our own homes or in our wider communities.

Veterans and patriots can draw inspiration from the soldiers who filled the jars at Jesus' command, illustrating obedience and sense of duty. Their task, simple yet necessary, facilitated Jesus' first public miracle. It's a reminder that even our seemingly small contributions can have a profound impact when aligned with divine will.

There is also a profound, though often understated, lesson in the transformation process. Jesus chose something as mundane as water and turned it into wine of exceptional quality. This transformation is an invitation for us to consider how God can take the ordinariness of our human lives and infuse it with divine purpose, making us vessels of His miraculous power.

As theologians and philosophers, the subtleties of this miracle beckon us to delve deeper into its layers of meaning. Is not the transformation of water into wine also a discourse on the Eucharist? The wine, symbolizing Christ's blood shed for humanity, is a prefiguration of the Last Supper where Jesus states, "This is my blood of the new testament, which is shed for many for the remission of sins" (Matt. 26:28). The Wedding at Cana serves as an early foreshadowing of the ultimate sacrifice on Calvary, setting the stage for the salvific plan of God to unfold.

In contemplating this mystery, we also gain insight into the relational aspect of Christ's ministry. Jesus' miracle at a wedding adds depth to our understanding of His desire to sanctify human relationships. It is through these divine-human interactions that God's plan continues to unfold. Jesus, by performing this miracle, blesses not only the bride and groom but all attendees, indicating that divine intervention can elevate the human experience to realms previously unimagined.

Finally, as we meditate on this luminous mystery, we are beckoned to see it as an affirmation of faith. Just as the servants who filled the jars took a leap of faith, so too are we called to trust in Jesus' timing and provision. The Wedding at Cana reminds us that even when it appears that "there is no wine"—be it joy, hope, or sustenance in our lives—God's grace is always poised to provide abundantly.

In conclusion, meditating on the Wedding at Cana offers a manifold of spiritual insights. It invites us to reflect on the sanctity of marriage, the power of Mary's intercession, the abundance of God's grace, and the transformative nature of Christ's presence. Whether we are involved in ecclesiastical duties, theological studies, or patriotic service, the lessons from this miracle guide us in our continual journey towards a deeper, fuller manifestation of faith in our daily lives.

## Contemplations on the Proclamation of the Kingdom

The Proclamation of the Kingdom of God is a profound mystery that radiates with hope and divine purpose. It represents the moment when Jesus of Nazareth, the Messiah, began to unveil the Kingdom of Heaven to mankind with His words and His works. "The time is fulfilled, and the kingdom of God is at hand: repent ye, and believe the gospel" (Mark 1:15). Heed these powerful words—the clarion call to a new era, where the reign of God intersects with human existence, inviting all to conversion and faith.

In considering the Proclamation of the Kingdom, we must first reflect on the nature of the Kingdom itself. This Kingdom is not of this world, nor does it conform to worldly expectations of power and grandeur. It is a Kingdom characterized by righteousness, peace, and joy in the Holy Spirit (Rom. 14:17). Jesus illustrated the Kingdom with simple yet profound parables—the mustard seed that grows into the largest of garden plants, the yeast that leavens the whole batch of dough, the treasure hidden in a field, and the pearl of great price (Matt. 13:31-46). Each parable reveals a facet of the Kingdom's mystery and magnificence.

The Kingdom of God is both present and future. Jesus inaugurated it with His Incarnation, life, and ministry, but it will reach its consummation at His Second Coming. This duality presents a theological and existential tension for the faithful, who live in the already-but-not-yet tension of the Kingdom. We are called to labor in this divine enterprise, planting seeds of justice, love, and mercy, confident that our efforts will bear eternal fruit.

One of the most poignant aspects of the Proclamation of the Kingdom is the Beatitudes, the heart of Jesus' Sermon on the Mount (Matt. 5:3-12). Here, Jesus subverts human expectations by blessing the poor in spirit, those who mourn, the meek, and those who hunger and thirst for righteousness. "Blessed are the merciful: for they shall obtain mercy. Blessed are the pure in heart: for they shall see God" (Matt. 5:7-8). The Beatitudes outline the characteristics of Kingdom citizens, creating a blueprint for holiness, justice, and compassion.

As Knights, Veterans, and Patriots, we find particularly relevant the call to active engagement in our world's temporal realities while remaining oriented toward the eternal Kingdom. We are to defend the defenseless, promote liberty and justice, and bear witness to the transformative power of grace. Yet, our motivation should always be anchored in a transcendent vision that Christ revealed—a Kingdom where love reigns supreme and every tear is wiped away (Rev. 21:4).

Priests and theologians often grapple with the tension between the sacred and the secular. In proclaiming the Kingdom, Jesus did not withdraw from the world; He engaged with it profoundly. He healed the sick, forgave the sinner, challenged the unjust, and comforted the sorrowful. His actions were unequivocally signs of the Kingdom breaking into history. The miracles performed by Jesus—curing the blind, raising the dead, and casting out demons—are not merely displays of divine power. They signal the advent of a new order where God's will is manifest "on earth, as it is in heaven" (Matt. 6:10).

Central to understanding the Proclamation of the Kingdom is repentance and conversion. John the Baptist prepared the way, preaching a baptism of repentance for the forgiveness of sins (Mark 1:4). When Jesus speaks of the Kingdom, He calls for a radical reorientation of life, not just a moral adjustment but a profound spiritual metamorphosis. "Except a man be born again, he cannot see the kingdom of God" (John 3:3). This second birth entails a relationship with Christ—a continual dying to the old self and rising to new life in Him (Rom. 6:4-8).

Philosophers and theologians have long deliberated on the nature of the Kingdom, exploring its implications for ethics, society, and personal sanctity. Yet, Jesus' own approach was accessible and relational. He spoke to fishermen, tax collectors, and sinners, inviting them into a community grounded in God's love. "I am come that they might have life, and that they might have it more abundantly" (John 10:10). These words encapsulate the essence of His mission.

Devotional meditation on the Proclamation of the Kingdom should propel us towards a deeper commitment to live out the Gospel values. It should rekindle our hope in the face of despair, inspire us to love amid hatred, and give us courage to advocate for justice where there is oppression. Remember Jesus' assurance: "Fear not, little flock; for it is your Father's good pleasure to give you the kingdom" (Luke 12:32). This divine promise strengthens us as we strive to embody the Kingdom in our daily lives.

Ultimately, the Kingdom of God demands our active participation and radical trust. As Knights of Columbus and faithful Catholics, we must take seriously the call to be ambassadors of this Kingdom, champions of truth, and stewards of divine grace. The Proclamation of the Kingdom, then, is not merely a historical event but an enduring and ever-relevant invitation to align our lives with God's salvific plan.

## Insights on the Transfiguration

The Transfiguration is a luminous flash of divine revelation in the journey of our Lord, an ethereal moment where the mortal veil is lifted, revealing a fleeting glance of the heavenly glory inherent in the Messiah. It's a transcendent event where human nature and divine glory intersect, connecting the realms of the temporal and the eternal in the person of Jesus Christ. We, as followers of Christ, find in this event not just a moment of awe but a depth of theological insight that speaks volumes about our faith, our destiny, and the nature of God's kingdom.

The Gospel accounts detail the Transfiguration with vivid imagery. Jesus ascends a high mountain with Peter, James, and John, and there, His appearance changes. "His face did shine as the sun, and his raiment was white as the light" (Matt. 17:2). This transformation is not just an embellishment; it is a profound manifestation of Jesus' divine nature. It serves as an assurance to the apostles and to us that Jesus is not merely a teacher or a prophet but is indeed the Son of God, radiant with divine splendor.

Mountains in Scripture often symbolize closeness to God, a place set apart for divine encounters. Just as Moses encountered God on Mount Sinai and Elijah heard the still small voice on Mount Horeb, Jesus' mountaintop transfiguration places Him in the context of divine revelation and marks Him as the fulfillment of the Law and the prophets. The presence of Moses and Elijah during the Transfiguration underscores this point, illustrating the continuity and culmination of the Old Testament in the person of Jesus Christ.

Let's contemplate the reaction of the apostles, who beheld this divine vision. Despite their initial fear and confusion, we recognize the privileged glimpse of glory they were granted. Peter's instinctive yet impetuous offer to build tabernacles (Matt. 17:4) for Jesus, Moses, and Elijah reveals his misunderstanding but also his deep desire to prolong this holy moment. It's a testimony to the human longing for the sacred, a longing that each one of us experiences.

The voice of the Father punctuates this divine revelation: "This is my beloved Son, in whom I am well pleased; hear ye him" (Matt. 17:5). These words not only affirm Jesus' identity but also direct our attention to Him as the ultimate revelation of God. Therefore, the

Transfiguration is more than a moment of glory; it is a divine command to listen to Jesus, to follow His teachings, and to trust in His ultimate plan for salvation. Such an imperative reaffirms the importance of Christ's words in our daily lives.

From a theological perspective, the Transfiguration prefigures the resurrection and glorification of Jesus. The dazzling light that envelops Christ is a foretaste of His resurrected form, providing a preview to the disciples of the triumph that will overcome the impending crucifixion. This event strengthens their faith, preparing them for the trials they will soon face and assuring them of the glory that lies beyond the cross. It is a beacon of hope, illuminating the path through suffering to the promise of eternal life.

Moreover, the Transfiguration provides profound eschatological insights. It symbolizes the promised transformation that awaits all believers. As Paul writes, "who shall change our vile body, that it may be fashioned like unto his glorious body" (Phil. 3:21). This isn't a distant, abstract hope but a tangible future reality. The encounter witnessed by Peter, James, and John assures us that our frail human nature will one day be transformed to share in Christ's divine glory. It's a call to live our lives in the light of this future resurrection, shaping our actions, hopes, and aspirations.

One can't ponder the Transfiguration without reflecting on the role of prayer in this divine encounter. Jesus ascends the mountain to pray, underscoring the transformative power of communion with God. It was in this moment of prayer that His divine nature was unveiled, reminding us of the potential for transformation in our own lives through earnest, heartfelt prayer. As we draw nearer to God, His light can also illuminate the darkest corners of our lives, leading to our own spiritual transfiguration.

For Roman Catholics, the Transfiguration is also richly connected to the liturgical life of the Church. The feast of the Transfiguration invites us yearly to meditate on this mystery, but more than that, every celebration of the Eucharist is a participation in divine glory. In the Holy Sacrifice of the Mass, the veil between heaven and earth is lifted, and we receive the radiant presence of Christ in the Eucharist, mirroring the divine encounter atop the high mountain. This ongoing liturgical experience invites us to live in perpetual awareness of Christ's glory.

Furthermore, reflecting on the Transfiguration beckons us to recognize the importance of moments of spiritual clarity in our own faith journeys. These moments, akin to mountaintop experiences, offer us glimpses of God's infinite love and beauty, often encountered during retreats, profound prayer sessions, or impactful spiritual readings. Just as the apostles carried the memory of the Transfiguration with them, these spiritual high points fortify our faith, sustaining us during times of trial and darkness.

The luminous glow of the Transfiguration also invites contemplation on the interior life and holiness. Saints and mystics, drawing from this divine encounter, emphasize the call to inner transformation. St. Paul exhorts us, "And be not conformed to this world: but be ye transformed by the renewing of your mind" (Rom. 12:2). This inward renewal, mirrored in the outward transfiguration of Christ, underscores that holiness is a process of becoming, a transformative journey toward the divine.

At its heart, the Transfiguration is a striking revelation of Christ's divine sonship and His role as the fulfillment of God's salvific plan. It calls for our response—listening to Christ, embracing His teachings, and allowing His light to transform our lives. As Knights of Columbus, priests, theologians, veterans, and lay faithful, the call to witness and emulate this divine transformation imbues our spiritual endeavors with greater purpose and urgency.

In conclusion, the Transfiguration serves as a luminous touchstone for our faith. It is a clarion call to live in hopeful anticipation of our own transformation, to engage in deep, prayerful communion with God, and to let Christ's radiant glory shine through our lives. Through the insights gathered from this divine encounter, may we be inspired to lead lives reflective of the divine light, bearing witness to the eternal truth and hope found in Christ Jesus.

## Thoughts on the Institution of the Eucharist

The Institution of the Eucharist stands as a monumental event in the life of Christ, resonating deeply within the hearts of the faithful. It is during the Last Supper that Jesus, in His boundless love, offered Himself as the perfect Sacrifice. By transforming bread and wine into His very Body and Blood, He instituted a new covenant with humanity. As He declares, "Take, eat; this is my body" (Matt. 26:26), we witness the profound mystery of our faith unfolding before us.

While gathered with His apostles, Jesus set into motion a deeply intimate act of divine condescension. In offering His Body and Blood, He prefigures the sacrificial act on Calvary, anticipating His Passion and enduring sacrifice for the salvation of mankind. This sublime truth is beautifully captured when He says, "This is my blood of the new testament, which is shed for many for the remission of sins" (Matt. 26:28). His words and actions at the Last Supper reveal the boundless depths of His mercy and love.

The Eucharist is both a memorial and a living reality. It is not merely a reenactment of the Last Supper but a participation in the Paschal Mystery itself. Here,

Christ's sacrifice is made present, not just symbolically, but in a very real and substantial way. The Catechism of the Catholic Church asserts, "The Eucharist is 'the source and summit of the Christian life'" (CCC, 1324). It is within the Mass that heaven meets earth, and time stands still. As we partake in the Eucharist, we join with the angels and saints, uniting ourselves to the eternal liturgy of heaven.

To truly grasp the Institution of the Eucharist, one must hold it as both a mystery to be adored and a gift to be received with utmost reverence. St. Paul exhorts the faithful in his first letter to the Corinthians, "For as often as ye eat this bread, and drink this cup, ye do shew the Lord's death till he come" (1 Cor. 11:26). This passage emphasizes the perpetual nature of Christ's sacrifice and the call to live in a state of grace, worthy of receiving so great a gift.

The theological significance of the Eucharist encompasses both Christ's presence and the transformative power it holds in the life of the believer. Through His real presence, Jesus nourishes the soul, strengthens the virtues, and fortifies the believer against sin. This intimate communion binds us to Him and, through Him, to one another. Our reception of the

Eucharist unites the Mystical Body of Christ, bringing us into deeper fellowship with our brothers and sisters in faith.

Moreover, as Catholics, we understand that the Eucharist is a foretaste of the heavenly banquet. It is an eschatological promise, a glimpse into the eternal joy that awaits us. In the Eucharist, the finite meets the infinite, and the temporal touches the eternal. In Revelation, John shares, "Blessed are they which are called unto the marriage supper of the Lamb" (Rev. 19:9). In this call, we find our hope and ultimate destiny, a hope renewed each time we approach the altar.

For priests, the celebration of the Eucharist is the supreme act of their vocation. In persona Christi, they consecrate the elements, acting as instruments of God's grace. This sacred duty underscores the immense responsibility placed on those who serve at the altar. They are the stewards of this divine mystery, entrusted to shepherd the faithful towards a fuller understanding and deeper reverence of the Sacrament.

As Knights of Columbus, veterans, and patriots, the Eucharist holds a special call to service. It challenges us to reflect Christ's sacrificial love in our daily lives. We are called to emulate His selflessness, to serve the marginalized, and to defend the dignity of every human life. In the Eucharist, we draw strength and courage to face the trials and tribulations of our earthly pilgrimage, ever mindful of the greater glory that awaits.

Philosophers and theologians have long pondered the Eucharist's profound mysteries. St. Thomas Aquinas declared, "To one who has faith, no explanation is necessary. To one without faith, no explanation is possible." This statement encapsulates the enigmatic nature of the Eucharist. It is something that defies human understanding yet invites us into a deeper relationship with God through faith. Theological musings may offer insights, but the heart of the Eucharist lies in the mystery of Christ's enduring presence.

The Institution of the Eucharist calls us to continual reflection and adoration. Each celebration is a moment of encounter with the Divine, an opportunity to renew our commitments, and a reminder of the eternal sacrifice that redeemed us. As Christ humbly offers Himself under the appearances of bread and wine, we are drawn into a deeper contemplation of His love and mercy.

In conclusion, the Eucharist is the foundation of our faith and the pinnacle of Christian worship. It demands a response of love, reverence, and full participation. As we approach the altar, let us do so with open hearts, ready to receive the immeasurable grace bestowed upon us through this most sacred Sacrament. Finally, let us echo the words of St. John the Baptist, "Behold the Lamb of God, which taketh away the sin of the world" (John 1:29). May our lives be a testament to the transformative power of the Eucharist, living witnesses to the love and mercy of our Lord and Savior, Jesus Christ.

## Chapter 3: The Sorrowful Mysteries

As we journey deeper into the mysteries of our faith, the Sorrowful Mysteries bring us face to face with the ultimate sacrifices made by our Lord Jesus Christ. These moments, filled with immense pain and anguish, beckon us to meditate on the profound love that propelled Him toward His destiny. Reflecting on the Agony in the Garden, we witness Jesus' agonizing prayer, where His sweat became as drops of blood (Luke 22:44), teaching us to seek communion with God in our darkest hours. The Scourging at the Pillar exposes the brutal reality of Jesus' suffering, reminding us of the physical and emotional wounds He bore for our salvation. With the Crowning of Thorns, we are called to recognize the mockery and humiliation He endured, emphasizing His Kingly dignity even in suffering. As we contemplate the Carrying of the Cross, we see Jesus' unwavering determination to fulfill His Father's will, encouraging us to embrace our own crosses with faith and perseverance. Finally, the Crucifixion stands as the pinnacle of God's love for humanity, where Christ's sacrificial death offers redemption, urging us to live lives of gratitude and devotion. "Father, forgive them; for they know not what they do" (Luke 23:34) echoes as a testament to the boundless mercy offered to all mankind. May these solemn reflections inspire us to draw closer to the heart of Jesus, embracing His sorrow as the pathway to our redemption and eternal joy.

## Reflections on the Agony in the Garden

In the stillness of Gethsemane, we witness a moment of profound human and divine convergence, where Jesus, the God-Man, experiences the depths of human agony. This episode, nestled in the heart of the Sorrowful Mysteries, invites us to enter into the silent groves of the Garden and contemplate the intense suffering Christ endures for our salvation. As we reflect on this mystery, we are not merely spectators; we are called to unite our own trials and tribulations with His, finding solace and strength in His example.

Jesus' agony in the garden is marked by His poignant prayer to the Father. "Father, if thou be willing, remove this cup from me: nevertheless not my will, but thine, be done" (Luke 22:42). His words resonate with anyone who has faced overwhelming suffering and sought relief, yet ultimately surrendered to God's will. Jesus' submission to the Father's will, despite the torment that awaits Him, teaches us about the true nature of obedience and trust in divine providence. This act of surrender is not passive but an active choice made in love and faith.

The Gospels paint a vivid picture of the emotional and physical anguish that Jesus endures. The very thought of the impending passion causes Him to sweat blood, a rare medical condition known as hematidrosis, indicative of extreme stress. This physiological response underscores the reality of Jesus' humanity; He is not immune to fear or suffering. By experiencing this agony, He fully enters into the human condition, offering a profound source of comfort for those who suffer. When we find ourselves grappling with our own fears and anxieties, we can turn to Jesus in Gethsemane, knowing that He understands our plight intimately.

Jesus' request for His disciples to "watch and pray" (Matt. 26:41) is a call to vigilance and prayerfulness in our spiritual journey. Despite their close relationship with Christ, the disciples succumb to sleep, failing to provide the support Jesus seeks. Their fatigue contrasts starkly with the intense alertness and vigilance He displays. This moment challenges us to examine our own spiritual lethargy. Are we awake and attentive to the presence of God in our lives, especially in times of trial, or do we, like the disciples, often fall asleep when our vigilance is needed most?

In their failure, the disciples reflect our own weaknesses and the ease with which we can falter. However, Jesus' response to their drowsiness is not one of anger but of gentle exhortation. "The spirit indeed is willing, but the flesh is weak" (Matt. 26:41). These words serve as both an acknowledgment of our human frailties and an encouragement to persevere. It is a reminder that prayer and vigilance fortify us against the onslaught of temptation and spiritual complacency.

As Jesus prays, He is visited by an angel who offers Him strength (Luke 22:43). This celestial comforter signifies that even in our darkest moments, God does not abandon us. Divine aid is always at hand, often arriving through unexpected avenues. The presence of the angel reassures us that God's grace is sufficient for us, even when we feel utterly alone. It is a testament to God's unwavering commitment to sustain us, especially in our most vulnerable moments.

The agony in the garden also invites us to consider the weight of our sins and their impact on Christ. Jesus is not merely anticipating the physical sufferings of the cross; He is also bearing the spiritual burden of the world's sins. The thought of becoming sin for us (2 Cor. 5:21) and experiencing separation from the Father causes Him indescribable anguish. This realization should drive us to a deeper appreciation of the gravity of sin and the price Jesus paid for our redemption. It calls us to sincere repentance and a commitment to live in accordance with His teachings.

In reflecting on Jesus' agony, we are also called to emulate His perseverance. Despite the overwhelming burden, Jesus does not turn away from His mission. His unwavering resolve to fulfill the Father's will, even in the face of great suffering, serves as a powerful model for our own lives. In times of trial, we can draw strength from His example, knowing that perseverance in faith and obedience ultimately leads to victory and resurrection.

The garden of Gethsemane, therefore, becomes a place of profound transformation. Here, Jesus transforms His agony into the beginning of our salvation. His acceptance of the cup He is given marks the commencement of His passion, a journey that leads to the cross but culminates in the resurrection. For us, it is a reminder that our sufferings, when united with Christ's, can also be transformative. They can become channels of grace, leading us closer to God and to the fulfillment of His will in our lives.

Moreover, the agony in the garden teaches us about the nature of true companionship and solidarity in suffering. Jesus turns to His closest friends in His moment of need, seeking their proximity and prayers. He does not seek to suffer alone, highlighting the importance of community in the Christian life. In our own lives, we are called to support one another in times of distress, offering our presence, prayers, and love. By doing so, we embody the compassion of Christ and create a tangible manifestation of God's love here on earth.

Ultimately, this mystery reveals the profound depth of Christ's love for humanity. His willingness to endure such intense agony for our sake is a testament to His boundless love and mercy. It calls us to respond to His love with gratitude, devotion, and a renewed commitment to live out our faith. As we meditate on the agony in the garden, let us allow our hearts to be moved by Christ's sacrifice and inspired to embrace our own crosses with courage and hope.

In uniting our sufferings with Christ's agony, we partake in the redemptive act of love that transforms pain into a path to salvation. This mystery encourages us to find meaning in our trials and to trust that, through them, we are being perfected in God's love. It is an invitation to enter into deeper communion with Jesus, who, in His moment of greatest suffering, shows us the path to eternal life.

## Meditations on the Scourging at the Pillar

As we immerse ourselves in the second Sorrowful Mystery, the Scourging at the Pillar, let us direct our minds and hearts to the profound suffering of our Lord Jesus Christ. This moment, marked by brutality and pain, holds a treasure of grace and insight for us.

Picture the scene: Jesus, the Son of God, bound to a cold, unyielding pillar, subjected to the merciless lashes of the Roman soldiers. Their whips, cruel instruments of torture, tore into His flesh, each stripe a manifestation of the sins He bore on behalf of humanity. As foretold in Isaiah, "He was wounded for our transgressions, He was bruised for our iniquities: the chastisement of our peace was upon Him; and with His stripes we are healed" (Isa. 53:5).

In this act of scourging, Jesus not only endured physical agony but also experienced the depths of human cruelty and indifference. He absorbed the worst of human sinfulness, displaying immense fortitude and divine love. His silence in the midst of such suffering reminds us of the lamb led to the slaughter, "And as a sheep before her shearers is dumb, so He openeth not His mouth" (Isa. 53:7). He who could command legions of angels chose to endure, teaching us the power of meekness and the redemptive scope of suffering accepted in love.

Contemplating this mystery, we are invited to reflect on our own experiences of suffering and sacrifice. Do we endure our trials with patience and trust in God's providence? Or do we rebel and complain against the burdens we face? Let us take to heart St. Paul's exhortation: "But we glory in tribulations also: knowing that tribulation worketh patience; and patience, experience; and experience, hope" (Rom. 5:3-4). Our pains have meaning when united with Christ's own Passion.

The scourging also embodies a cry against the injustices of the world. Jesus, innocent and pure, submitted to an unjust punishment. This should stir within us a zeal for justice and a compassion for the oppressed and the marginalized. As Knights of Columbus and as devout Catholics, we are called to defend the poor, the voiceless, and the downtrodden in society. We are reminded of Christ's teaching: "Verily I say unto you, Inasmuch as ye have done it unto one of the least of these my brethren, ye have done it unto me" (Matt. 25:40).

The sight of the Savior's torn and bleeding body, while heart-wrenching, offers a profound lesson in divine love. By willingly accepting such torture, Jesus demonstrates the depth of His love for mankind, a love that knows no bounds. As St. John states, "Greater love hath no man than this, that a man lay down his life for his friends" (John 15:13). Jesus' sacrifice is the ultimate expression of this profound truth. It challenges us to embody this love in our relationships, to forgive those who wrong us, and to love our enemies as He has commanded.

Moreover, Jesus' suffering at the pillar calls us to a deeper sense of humility and acknowledgment of our sinfulness. Each lash He bore is a testament to the weight of our sins. Recognizing this, let us approach the Sacrament of Reconciliation with sincere contrition and a firm resolve to amend our lives. "If we confess our sins, He is faithful and just to forgive us our sins, and to cleanse us from all unrighteousness" (1 John 1:9).

Reflecting on the harsh reality of the scourging, we also recognize the enormous cost of our redemption. The price was not paid in silver or gold, but in the precious blood of Christ, "as of a lamb without blemish and without spot" (1 Pet. 1:19). This awareness should fill our hearts with gratitude and inspire us to live lives worthy of such a sacrifice, striving for holiness and righteousness in all our actions.

The scourging at the pillar, while an event of deep sorrow and pain, opens a door to a greater understanding of God's unfathomable love and mercy. It beckons us to respond with heartfelt devotion, courageous faith, and unwavering commitment to follow in the footsteps of Christ, even unto suffering. It is a call to join our pains with His, transforming them into a source of grace and redemption for the world.

In conclusion, let us remember the scourging at the pillar as not only a scene of immense suffering but as a testament to the boundless love and redemptive sacrifice of our Lord Jesus Christ. When we meditate on this mystery, may our hearts be filled with a deeper compassion, a stronger commitment to justice, and a courageous embrace of our own sufferings. Let us strive to live by the words of St. Paul: "I am crucified with Christ: nevertheless I live; yet not I, but Christ liveth in me" (Gal. 2:20). Thus, in our every trial, we find unity with our Savior, and in every stripe, we uncover God's enduring mercy.

## Contemplations on the Crowning with Thorns

The Crowning with Thorns is one of the most agonizing episodes in the Passion of Christ. It stands as an emblem of not just physical suffering, but emotional and spiritual travail. Imagine, for a moment, the soldiers' brutal mockery. They did not merely seek to cause pain but to debase and humiliate. The thorny crown, twisted together in cruel jest, was thrust upon the head of our Savior, each thorn piercing deeply, causing blood to flow down His sacred face. Through this particular sorrow, Christ accepted derision and disgrace for our sake, transforming these human acts of cruelty into a divine act of love.

In envisioning this sacred moment, one might be struck by the weight of the world's sins that pressed upon His holy brow. "And when they had platted a crown of thorns, they put it upon His head, and a reed in His right hand: and they bowed the knee before Him, and mocked Him, saying, Hail, King of the Jews!" (Matt. 27:29). This poignant scene depicts not only an excruciating physical pain, but a profound act of sacrificial love. Christ, in His innocence, bore the persecution that was meant for us. How do we comprehend such vast mercy?

As Roman Catholics, Knights of Columbus, and faithful adherents, we are called to meditate deeply upon this scene. The crowning of Jesus with thorns is not merely a historical event; it is a mirror reflecting our own tendencies to mock, diminish, and hurt one another. In our moments of honest reflection, we begin to see the thorns that we have placed on the heads of our brethren through our judgments, harsh words, and lack of compassion. Redemption begins when we recognize this and strive to amend our lives, choosing paths of charity and humility over arrogance and derision.

This contemplation also calls forth a spirit of patriotism grounded in virtue and sacrifice. Jesus' acceptance of the crown of thorns without retaliation is a lesson in true leadership and service. He did not lord His kingship over others; instead, He accepted suffering for the greater good. True patriotism involves loving and serving our country and our community with similar selflessness, bearing hardships for the sake of protecting and uplifting others.

Recall that Jesus, enduring the thorns, personified the virtues extolled in the Beatitudes. "Blessed are the meek: for they shall inherit the earth" (Matt. 5:5). Our Lord's nonviolent response to brutal scorn is the living embodiment of meekness, a lesson sorely needed in our world today. This event in His Passion teaches us that true strength lies not in physical might, but in spiritual resilience and profound humility.

Those who serve in the armed forces, veterans who have borne witness to the horrors of war, understand the sacrifices that come with protecting liberty and justice. The Crowning with Thorns can serve as a model for these brave souls. Just as Christ did not recoil from His mission, so too must soldiers and defenders of the faith exhibit courage and integrity, even in the face of adversity and ridicule. In this act, we find not only the call to endure suffering gracefully but also the hope of ultimate victory through perseverance.

Theologians and priests have long found in the Crowning with Thorns a profound theological richness. The intertwining of Christ's role as King and Sufferer deepens our comprehension of the Paschal Mystery. The crown, an instrument of torture, symbolizes His kingship inaugurated through sacrifice. His acceptance of humiliation reveals a regal dignity defined not by earthly splendor, but by sacrificial love. "Who, being in the form of God, thought it not robbery to be equal with

God: But made Himself of no reputation, and took upon Him the form of a servant" (Phil. 2:6-7).

Jesus' agony under the crown of thorns also invites a philosophical reflection on the nature of suffering and human dignity. The setting aside of His divine privileges to undergo human torment reveals volumes about the sanctity of human suffering. Through His Passion, He reassures us that our own sufferings, when united with His, become redemptive. Christ transforms our pain into a means of participating in His salvific mission, reminding us that dignity is found not in avoiding suffering but in embracing it for a higher purpose.

Thus, as we meditate upon this sorrowful mystery, we are called to imitate Christ's response to suffering. This includes enduring trials with patience, responding to offenses with forgiveness, and offering our own pains as sacrifices for the sanctification of others. Here, the theological meets the practical, urging us to follow in His footsteps in our daily encounters and struggles.

Each thorn that pierced the brow of Jesus was for the redemption of every man and woman, a piercing illustration of unwavering love. His silent endurance is a hymn of profound grace and patience. As we meditate upon His suffering, may we find the strength to face our own trials with a Christ-like heart, knowing that through Him, every thorn has purpose and every agony has meaning.

Furthermore, contemplating the Crowning with Thorns allows us to enter into a deeper dialogue with God about the nature of suffering and redemption. Scripture reminds us of the eternal impact of Christ's sacrifice: "Surely He hath borne our griefs, and carried our sorrows: yet we did esteem Him stricken, smitten of God, and afflicted" (Isa. 53:4). Here, Isaiah's prophecy reverberates through the corridors of time, finding fulfillment in the passion narrative.

Ultimately, the Crowning with Thorns invites us into an intimate relationship with Jesus. It calls us to sit with Him in His suffering, to console Him with our faithfulness, and to walk with Him on the path of love and redemption. This contemplation is not an end in itself, but a journey towards greater union with Christ, enabling us to manifest His love more profoundly in our world. Through this sacred mystery, may we learn to bear our own "thorns" with grace and offer them as gifts to our Lord, who wore the ultimate crown of suffering for the salvation of humanity.

## Insights on the Carrying of the Cross

The journey Jesus made from Pilate's court to Golgotha is a profound reflection on the human condition, suffering, and the redemptive power of sacrificial love. Imagine the scene: Jesus, already bruised and battered from the scourging, takes up His cross. It is not merely a piece of wood but a symbol of the weight of the world's sins. As He begins His walk, each step resonates with divine purpose and immense love.

Meeting His mother along the way, a moment that is both heart-wrenching and illuminating, we witness the intersection of divine mission and human emotion. Mary's presence, her silent suffering and strength, underlines the unique bond between Jesus and His mother. This encounter speaks volumes about the role of Mary in the salvation narrative, offering a powerful image of faith and courage amidst unimaginable pain.

Simon's act of carrying Jesus' cross reminds us of our call to empathy and assistance toward those who bear heavy burdens. "And as they led him away, they laid hold upon one Simon, a Cyrenian, coming out of the country, and on him they laid the cross, that he might bear it after Jesus" (Luke 23:26). Simon's reluctant yet pivotal role in the Passion narrative exemplifies how God often calls us to help carry the crosses of others, even when we least expect it, teaching us about solidarity and compassion.

The interactions with the women of Jerusalem add another layer to this sorrowful journey. Jesus, ever the shepherd even in His agony, pauses to offer words of warning and comfort. "Daughters of Jerusalem, weep not for me, but weep for yourselves, and for your children" (Luke 23:28). This interaction emphasizes Jesus' ceaseless concern for others, reinforcing His boundless love and the prophetic nature of His suffering.

The carrying of the cross, though steeped in physical and spiritual torment, is not only an act of redemption but also a call to discipleship. Jesus invites each of us to take up our own crosses, to follow Him in paths that may be arduous but ultimately lead to eternal life. "Then said Jesus unto his disciples, If any man will come after me, let him deny himself, and take up his cross, and follow me" (Matt. 16:24). This injunction to carry our own crosses encourages a life of virtue, sacrifice, and reflection on our purpose within God's plan.

It is helpful to remember that the cross was not solely a symbol of suffering but also one of hope and transformation. As Jesus carried His cross, He was paving the way for the triumph of life over death, light over darkness, and love over hate. The cross, initially an instrument of execution, became the universally recognized emblem of Christian faith and the ultimate testament to God's love for humanity.

Moreover, the carrying of the cross is a poignant reminder that suffering is an inextricable part of the human experience. Whether it is physical pain, emotional distress, or spiritual struggle, all are invited to unite their suffering with Jesus. This act of union can transform our pain into redemptive experiences, opening channels of grace and deepening our intimacy with Christ.

The via dolorosa, or "way of sorrows," walked by Christ sets an eternal example for all believers. The path was not chosen for convenience or to showcase power but to manifest the profound truth of sacrificial love. The physical strain and emotional burden embodied in each step provide a universal template for facing our challenges with faith and resilience.

Drawing on the wisdom from saints and theologians, it becomes evident that the carrying of the cross invites reflection not just on Christ's Passion but on personal growth through suffering. Saints like John of the Cross have written extensively on the purifying power of trials: "In the Cross alone is the soul purified and receives its greatest richness and delight" (St. John of the Cross). This mystical insight reveals how adversities, when embraced with faith, can refine the soul and draw it closer to Divine love.

For many veterans and patriots, the carrying of the cross has special resonance. It symbolizes ultimate sacrifice, not unlike the sacrifices made in the service of one's country. The discipline, courage, and dedication seen in the lives of soldiers find a celestial parallel in the path Jesus trod. Each soldier's story of valor and sacrifice can be mirrored in the Passion narrative, fostering a deeper appreciation for duty, honor, and love for others.

Priests, theologians, and educators find, in this mystery, rich material for teaching and preaching about Christ's salvific mission. The carrying of the cross encapsulates crucial theological themes such as atonement, redemption, and divine love. These themes not only nourish the intellect but also inspire spiritual renewal and commitment among the faithful.

As we meditate on Jesus' journey to Calvary, we see more than just historical or spiritual narrative; we see a mirror for our struggles and a model for our endurance. The cross teaches us that through perseverance and unwavering faith, we can transform our trials into sources of strength, hope, and ultimate joy. This transformation reflects the final victory that awaits all believers who take up their crosses and follow Christ.

In conclusion, the carrying of the cross is a powerful testament to Christ's love and the human capacity for strength through suffering. It calls us to empathy, demands our courage, and strengthens our faith. As we walk our own paths of sorrow, let us take inspiration from Jesus' journey, knowing that every cross we bear is an opportunity to grow closer to Him and participate in the mystery of our redemption.

## Thoughts on the Crucifixion

The crucifixion of our Lord Jesus Christ is a profound and harrowing mystery that lies at the heart of our faith. As Roman Catholics, it's crucial for us to meditate deeply on this sorrowful event, to understand and appreciate the immense love and sacrifice it represents. When Jesus was nailed to the cross, He didn't just endure physical torment; He carried the weight of the world's sins, bridging the chasm between humanity and God.

The crucifixion is a stark reminder of the brutal extent to which Christ went to redeem us. In the Gospel of Luke, it is written, "And when they were come to the place, which is called Calvary, there they crucified him, and the malefactors, one on the right hand, and the other on the left" (Luke 23:33). This vivid imagery serves to bring to light the setting of His suffering and the gravity of the moment. Jesus, the sinless Lamb of God, was crucified alongside criminals, portraying the depth of His humility and solidarity with the lowliest of sinners.

One cannot contemplate the crucifixion without being moved by the physical agony Christ endured. His beaten and scourged body carried to the hill of Golgotha, and there, with nails piercing His hands and feet, He was lifted up on the cross. The agony was excruciating, yet out of such suffering, the greatest act of love and salvation was manifest. As Catholics, reflecting on this mystery should evoke a transformation within us, a call to embrace our crosses with faith and trust in God's greater plan.

Yet, the physical pain was only one dimension of Jesus' suffering. He faced profound emotional and spiritual anguish, encapsulated in His cry, "My God, my God, why hast thou forsaken me?" (Matt. 27:46). This moment of utter desolation, a feeling of abandonment even by His Father, highlights His complete and total identification with the human condition. It is a potent reminder that in our darkest moments, Jesus understands our pain, having walked that path Himself.

Reflecting on Jesus' words spoken from the cross deepens our understanding of His love and mission. The words "Father, forgive them; for they know not what they do" (Luke 23:34) resonate with mercy and compassion. Despite the cruelty of His executioners, Jesus pleaded for their forgiveness, exemplifying the boundless mercy that characterizes His divine nature.

This call to forgiveness challenges us to extend that same mercy to others in our lives, advocating for reconciliation over revenge.

As Knights of Columbus, veterans, and patriots, meditating on the crucifixion should inspire us to live lives of sacrificial service. The ultimate sacrifice made by Jesus calls us to emulate His selflessness in our endeavors, to stand up for justice, truth, and compassion regardless of the personal cost. Each time we contemplate the cross, let it spur us to acts of kindness and service, reflecting the light of Christ in our communities and nations.

Furthermore, the presence of the Blessed Virgin Mary at the foot of the cross serves as a poignant reflection of maternal love and sorrow. As she beheld her Son's suffering, Mary's heart was pierced with a sword of grief (Luke 2:35). Her silent courage and unwavering faith provide a powerful example for all believers. Turning to Mary in our meditations can offer us consolation and strength, reminding us that we are never alone in our suffering.

Looking at the crucifixion through a theological lens, it illuminates the mystery of redemption. The cross is not merely a symbol of suffering but one of victory—victory over sin and death. "But God commendeth his love toward us, in that, while we were yet sinners, Christ died for us" (Rom. 5:8). This profound truth underscores the unconditional love God has for us, a love that should compel us to live righteously and fervently in our faith.

For theologians and philosophers, the crucifixion invites deep exploration into the concepts of sacrifice, atonement, and divine justice. It poses questions about the human condition, the problem of evil, and the nature of God's love and justice. In pondering these mysteries, we grow in our understanding of divine truths and are better equipped to articulate the reason for our hope to those who seek answers.

As priests and religious, the crucifixion is central to our ministry and teaching. It is at the core of the Eucharist, where Christ's sacrifice is made present and real for the faithful. Each Mass allows us to enter into the mystery of the crucifixion, commemorating and participating in the sacrificial love of Christ. It is both our duty and privilege to guide the faithful in understanding and living out the implications of the crucifixion in their daily lives.

The passion and crucifixion of Jesus stand as a beacon of hope amid despair, a testament to the triumph of love over hatred, and life over death. It's a story that has the power to convert souls and transform lives when truly meditated upon. By contemplating the crucifixion, we draw nearer to the heart of God, understanding that through suffering, redemption is achieved, and through the cross, victory is won.

In our meditations, let us remember that the cross is not the end of the story. Beyond the crucifixion lies the resurrection, the ultimate demonstration of Christ's power and victory over death. Thus, as we ponder the sorrow and sacrifice of Good Friday, we should also hold fast to the promise and hope of Easter Sunday. The crucifixion, therefore, becomes a wellspring of faith, a reminder that through trials and tribulations, there emerges a promise of new life and everlasting joy.

## Chapter 4: The Glorious Mysteries

As we immerse ourselves in the Glorious Mysteries, the radiant promise of Christ's triumph over death lights our path. "I am the resurrection, and the life: he that believeth in me, though he were dead, yet shall he live" (John 11:25). Reflect upon the Resurrection, the cornerstone of our faith, infusing hope into the darkest corners of human struggle. Meditate on the Ascension, where Christ ascends, paving the way for our eternal destiny. Contemplate the Descent of the Holy Spirit, the Comforter who fortifies us with divine grace and wisdom. Consider the Assumption of Mary, a testimony to the purity and dignity bestowed upon the Mother of God. Finally, visualize the Coronation of Mary, where she is exalted as Queen of Heaven and Earth, magnifying the Lord who "hath scattered the proud in the imagination of their hearts" (Luke 1:51). Through these mysteries, our souls are stirred, our faith deepened, and our service to God and country renewed with a fervent spirit of love and sacrifice.

## Reflections on the Resurrection

The Resurrection of Jesus Christ stands as the cornerstone of Christian faith, a beacon of hope and an unparalleled testament to the divine power of God. In meditating on this glorious mystery, we draw strength from the triumph over death and sin, understanding that the Resurrection is not merely an event in history but a continual spiritual reality that pervades our lives.

In the early dawn of that first Easter Sunday, as related by Saint Luke, the women who went to the tomb were met with an astonishing revelation: "Why seek ye the living among the dead? He is not here, but is risen" (Luke 24:5-6). These words resonate through the ages, reminding us that Jesus has conquered the grave. The stone that was rolled away from the tomb becomes a metaphor for the barriers and burdens in our own lives that can be removed through faith in Christ.

To ponder the Resurrection is to reflect on the new beginnings it heralds. For those who might feel ensnared by past errors or trapped by current struggles, the Resurrection offers a promise of renewal. This new life is vividly illustrated by the transformation seen in the Apostles. From fear and doubt, they were emboldened by the sight of the Risen Lord, who appeared to them saying, "Peace be unto you" (John 20:19). This peace, a gift from the Resurrected Christ, assures us that we too can overcome our tribulations.

The Resurrection underpins the doctrine of life after death, a central tenet for Roman Catholics. It is through Christ's victory over death that we, too, are promised eternal life. Saint Paul asserts, "But now is Christ risen from the dead, and become the firstfruits of them that slept" (1 Cor. 15:20). This profound truth calls us to live our present lives with an eternal perspective, grounding our daily actions and decisions in the hope of the life to come.

For Knights of Columbus, veterans, priests, theologians, and laypersons alike, the Resurrection encourages active participation in the mission of the Church. Just as the Apostles were sent forth to proclaim the Good News, we too are called to be witnesses of the Resurrection in our communities. This entails not just verbal proclamation but living out the Gospel through acts of charity, justice, and love.

Reflect also on the appearances of the Risen Christ. To Mary Magdalene, He said, "Touch me not; for I am not yet ascended to my Father" (John 20:17). This encounter symbolizes the personal nature of our faith journey. Christ knows each of us intimately and calls us by name. To encounter the resurrected Christ is to experience a profound personal conversion, as seen in Mary's transformation from sorrow to joy.

Moreover, the walk to Emmaus, as narrated in the Gospel of Luke, offers a powerful example of how Jesus meets us in our uncertainty and despair. The disciples, weighed down by confusion, are unaware of His presence until the breaking of the bread. "And their eyes were opened, and they knew him" (Luke 24:31). This journey serves as a metaphor for our own faith journeys and the Eucharist's pivotal role in recognizing Jesus in our midst.

The Resurrection is also a call to evangelize. Post-resurrection, Christ's instruction was clear: "Go ye into all the world, and preach the gospel to every creature" (Mark 16:15). This imperative transcends time and context, urging us to share the transformative power of Jesus's Resurrection actively. In doing so, we not only reinforce our faith but also invite others to partake in the joy and peace that only the risen Christ can provide.

In our reflections, let us not overlook the deep theological implications of Christ's victory over death. The Resurrection validates Christ's divinity and the truth of His teachings. Saint Paul's words are poignant: "And if Christ be not risen, then is our preaching vain, and your faith is also vain" (1 Cor. 15:14). The Resurrection is the fulfillment of Old Testament prophecies and a testament to God's faithfulness and omnipotence.

This glorious mystery also illuminates the pathway to holiness and virtue. The new life brought forth by the Resurrection is a call to "put off the old man with his deeds; and have put on the new man, which is renewed in knowledge after the image of him that created him" (Col. 3:9-10). In practical terms, this means striving to embody the virtues of humility, patience, and love in our daily lives.

Contemplate too the communal aspect of the Resurrection. When Christ appeared to His disciples, He breathed on them and said, "Receive ye the Holy Ghost" (John 20:22). This act instituted the Church as the living body of Christ on earth. Through the Resurrection, we are united not only with Christ but also with each other in the mystical body of the Church.

This unity calls for mutual support, encouragement, and service within the Christian community.

Finally, the Resurrection impels us to look forward with hope and anticipation to our own resurrection at the end of time. "For if we believe that Jesus died and rose again, even so them also which sleep in Jesus will God bring with him" (1 Thes. 4:14). This eschatological hope should invigorate our lives, providing comfort in times of sorrow and inspiring us to live righteously.

In summation, our reflections on the Resurrection should inspire us to live in the light of Christ's victory, nurture our hope in eternal life, and commit ourselves to the mission of the Church. It is a mystery that perpetually renews our faith, transforms our actions, and fortifies our souls. As we meditate on this glorious event, let us rejoice with the words of the angel, "He is not here; for he is risen" (Matt. 28:6). Alleluia, alleluia!

## Meditations on the Ascension

As we delve into the Ascension, the second of the Glorious Mysteries, we find ourselves contemplating Jesus' rise to Heaven after His Resurrection. This event, rich with divine significance and human wonder, is emblematic of victory over sin and death. It serves as a profound testament to both Christ's divinity and the eternal promise bestowed upon mankind. As He ascends, so too are we called to lift our thoughts, actions, and spirits upwards, embracing the hope and eternal life He offers.

In the Acts of the Apostles, we read: "And when he had spoken these things, while they beheld, he was taken up; and a cloud received him out of their sight." (Acts 1:9) This majestic scene encapsulates both the physical departure of Christ and the spiritual anticipation of His return. The Ascension is a moment of joyous sorrow—joy in the fulfillment of God's promise and sorrow in the temporary physical separation from the Lord. Yet it is within this sorrow that the ultimate joy is promised: the descent of the Holy Spirit and the full establishment of God's Church on earth.

As Knights of Columbus and veterans, we understand the concept of service and sacrifice. Christ's Ascension was a proclamation of His mission accomplished, an assurance that His work on earth was complete, and that it would continue through those who believe in Him. He entrusts us with a divine commission, echoing His words, "Go ye therefore, and teach all nations, baptizing them in the name of the Father, and of the Son, and of the Holy Ghost." (Matt. 28:19) This command is a call for evangelization and embodies our duty to spread the Gospel with courage and fidelity.

Consider the Apostles, standing gazing at the heavens, their hearts mixed with amazement and trepidation. They were ordinary men called to perform an extraordinary mission. Through the strength of the Holy Spirit, they transformed the world. Their experience is a testament to what can be achieved when human frailty is united with divine grace. This harmonious unity is something veterans and patriots deeply comprehend; it reminds us that any undertaking, however monumental, can be fulfilled through divine aid and human resolve.

Christ's departure inaugurates a new era—the era of the Church. It's an era marked by the presence of the

Holy Spirit, who guides, empowers, and sanctifies. As priests and theologians often reflect, the Ascension is not just about Jesus leaving the earth, but about His continual presence in a new, sacramental form. The Church becomes Christ's body, and through its sacraments, the faithful experience His constant, sustaining presence. The Catechism of the Catholic Church beautifully articulates this, stating, "Christ's Ascension into heaven signifies his participation, in his humanity, in God's power and authority." (CCC 668)

To theologians and philosophers, the Ascension also poses a question of metaphysical importance: How can one be fully human and yet fully divine? This mystery must be approached not merely with the intellect but with a heart open to faith. The Apostles teach us that divine mysteries are not obstacles to understanding but pathways to deeper truth. Their unwavering faith, anchored in Christ's words and the promises of Scripture, serves as a beacon guiding our own spiritual journeys.

For the Roman Catholic faithful, the Ascension is a profound reminder of our heavenly destiny. "If ye then be risen with Christ, seek those things which are above, where Christ sitteth on the right hand of God." (Col.

3:1) The Ascension urges us to aspire towards our heavenly calling. It reminds us that earthly life is transient, a mere passage towards eternal communion with God. This heavenly perspective should influence our daily lives, prompting us to live with integrity, compassion, and a fervent desire to fulfill God's will.

Priests play a pivotal role in echoing the message of the Ascension. Through their ministry, they act as Christ's representatives, bridging the divine and earthly realms. Their vocation is a living example of a life dedicated to God's service, continuously inviting the faithful to lift their eyes and hearts to the heavens. The Ascension underscores the sanctity and lofty vocation of the priesthood, serving as an inspiration and goal for those called to this sacred office.

Throughout the centuries, saints and mystics have drawn profound insights from the Ascension. Saint John of the Cross meditated on the soul's ascent to God, an ascent mirrored in Christ's physical rising. This ascent isn't just an upward movement but a deepening of one's interior life, a continual striving towards spiritual perfection. The Ascension inspires us to recognize that our spiritual journey, though arduous, is part of a divine trajectory ending in glory and eternal union with God.

This mystery also holds deep patriotic significance. It challenges us to envision our national identity through the lens of faith. As patriots, we are called to aim for higher principles—justice, freedom, and true dignity for all, reflecting the divine order. Jesus' Ascension serves as a reminder that all governance should ultimately aim towards heavenly ideals. The principles of truth and justice are rooted in divine law, and it is our duty to strive for a society that mirrors God's kingdom on earth.

Moreover, the Ascension endows us with the knowledge that Christ, ascended and seated at the right hand of the Father, intercedes for us. "Who is he that condemneth? It is Christ that died, yea rather, that is risen again, who is even at the right hand of God, who also maketh intercession for us." (Rom. 8:34) This intercession is a constant source of hope and strength, especially in times of trial. For veterans and all who have experienced the trials of service, knowing that Christ intercedes on our behalf is profoundly consoling. It reassures us that no matter our struggles, we are never alone.

The Ascension also beckons us to cultivate a spirit of expectation. Just as the disciples awaited the coming of the Holy Spirit, so too must we live in hopeful anticipation of Christ's return. This eschatological awareness impels us to be vigilant and proactive in our faith. It's a reminder that our earthly endeavors, though fraught with challenges, are part of a larger divine plan. Every act of charity, every moment of witness, hastens the coming of God's kingdom.

In conclusion, the Ascension is not merely a historical event but an invitation to live in the fullness of Christ's promise. It calls us to engage in a heavenly orientation, transforming our lives by the power of the Holy Spirit. This mystery compels us to elevate our thoughts, live out our faith boldly, and carry forward Christ's mission on earth. As we meditate on the Ascension, let us recommit ourselves to seeking the things above, knowing that our ultimate home is with Christ in the heavenly realms.

May this reflection on the Ascension inspire us to live with hearts alight with hope, minds attuned to divine wisdom, and

## Contemplations on the Descent of the Holy Spirit

The Descent of the Holy Spirit marks a pivotal moment in the life of the early Church. With Jesus having ascended into heaven, the apostles found themselves in a state of both expectation and uncertainty. It was during the feast of Pentecost that their longing was fulfilled. As they gathered in the upper room, the promised Advocate came upon them like a rushing wind (Acts 2:1-4). It's an event rich in theological and spiritual significance, worthy of deep contemplation and reverent meditation.

The scene is both awe-inspiring and humbling. Picture the apostles, ordinary men with extraordinary missions, now filled with the Holy Spirit. Tongues of fire appeared and rested upon each of them. Imagine the surge of courage, wisdom, and divine insight that must have flooded their souls. Many of us encounter periods of doubt and fear in our own journeys, feeling unprepared or inadequate. When we reflect on the Descent of the Holy Spirit, we are reminded that divine strength and guidance are available to us, just as they were to the apostles.

The Holy Spirit's work didn't end at Pentecost; rather, it was the beginning of His active presence in the Church and in the hearts of the faithful. It's a timeless invitation for us to open ourselves to His transformative power. As Knights of Columbus, veterans, and patriots, we are called to defend and propagate our faith with the same fervor that ignited the apostles. Just as "they were all filled with the Holy Ghost, and began to speak with other tongues, as the Spirit gave them utterance" (Acts 2:4), we too can be instruments of God's will, ambassadors of His love and truth.

Consider the symbolism of the flame. Fire provides warmth, light, and purifies. The Holy Spirit as a flame signifies His role in illuminating our minds to the truths of faith, warming our hearts with divine love, and purifying our souls from sin. We are reminded of the prophet Isaiah's words: "The spirit of the Lord shall rest upon him, the spirit of wisdom and understanding, the spirit of counsel and might, the spirit of knowledge and of the fear of the Lord" (Isa. 11:2). These gifts of the Spirit are not just for the apostles but are available to all who seek them earnestly.

In the context of our current society, the messages and fruits of the Holy Spirit are critically needed. Wisdom, understanding, counsel, fortitude, knowledge, piety, and fear of the Lord can transform not only individuals but entire communities. Theological and philosophical understanding can become a bedrock for critical thinking and ethical discernment. As theologians and priests, you have the sacred duty to teach and interpret these mysteries, guiding the faithful towards a deeper relationship with God.

Moreover, the mission given to the apostles was clear and direct: to be witnesses "unto the uttermost part of the earth" (Acts 1:8). The Holy Spirit empowered them to preach, to heal, to build communities, and to bear witness to the resurrection of Christ. This ecclesial mission is echoed in our lives today. As patriots and veterans who have served with honor and distinction, reflect on how the Spirit communicates through acts of courage and service. How does your vocational calling resonate with the call to spread the Gospel?

When we read that "they were all with one accord in one place" (Acts 2:1), we see a profound unity among the apostles. This unity is an essential aspect of the work of the Holy Spirit. It calls for us to foster unity in our parishes, councils, and communities. The Spirit binds us together in love, making us one body in Christ despite our individual differences and backgrounds. Unity in the Spirit is a powerful testimony to the world of God's Kingdom.

Consider also the reaction of the crowd in Jerusalem. They were bewildered, amazed, and some even skeptical, not comprehending what they were witnessing (Acts 2:12-13). It's a poignant reminder that the message of the Gospel and the movements of the Holy Spirit can be both enlightening and confounding to the world. As we live out our faith, we must expect both acceptance and resistance. Our response should be rooted in the Spirit's gifts—wisdom to understand, fortitude to persevere, and charity to love even those who oppose us.

The story of Pentecost continues with Peter's powerful sermon, through which three thousand souls were converted (Acts 2:41). This moment signifies the fruitful outcome of yielding to the Holy Spirit. It shows how God can use our words and actions to bring about conversion and renewal. Whether you are a priest delivering a homily, a theologian writing a book, or a layperson sharing your faith, know that the Holy Spirit can amplify your efforts far beyond what you might imagine.

Lives transformed by the Spirit often reflect a radical shift in values, priorities, and behaviors. Think of the early Christian community described in Acts: "And they continued stedfastly in the apostles' doctrine and fellowship, and in breaking of bread, and in prayers" (Acts 2:42). It's a powerful blueprint for Christian living—rooted in teaching, fellowship, Eucharist, and prayer. As philosophers among you contemplate these foundational elements, recognize their enduring relevance and their ability to stir profound inner change.

Ultimately, reflecting on the Descent of the Holy Spirit encourages us to invite the Spirit into our daily lives. Ask for His guidance in your decisions, His comfort in your trials, and His joy in your blessings. Pray for a deeper outpouring of His gifts, that you may become a more effective instrument of His will. It's a journey of continual conversion and growth, one that brings us closer to the heart of God and unites us more fully with our fellow believers.

In closing this contemplation, let's echo the words of the psalmist: "Create in me a clean heart, O God; and renew a right spirit within me" (Ps. 51:10). May the Holy Spirit's descent not be just a historical event we commemorate, but a present reality we experience, transforming us into bold witnesses of Christ's saving love.

**Insights on the Assumption of Mary**

The Assumption of Mary, a celebrated belief among Roman Catholics, is an event marked by profound spiritual and theological implications. As we traverse "The Glorious Mysteries," it is essential to delve into the depths of this dogma, its biblical foundations, and its significance for believers today. The event of the Assumption, which asserts that Mary was taken up body and soul into heavenly glory at the end of her earthly life, serves as a testament to the ultimate victory over sin and death promised to all the faithful.

The Assumption is not explicitly detailed in the Scriptures, yet it draws heavily on biblical typology and tradition. For instance, the Song of Solomon provides a poetic glimpse of Mary: "Who is she that looketh forth as the morning, fair as the moon, clear as the sun, and terrible as an army with banners?" (Song of Solomon 6:10). This verse exemplifies the Church's view of Mary as a magnificent reflection of God's glory.

One of the parallels often drawn in support of the Assumption is the story of Elijah. Just as Elijah was taken up into heaven in a whirlwind (2 Kings 2:11), so too was Mary assumed. The absence of Mary's tomb or relics throughout Christian history further underscores the unique nature of her departure from this world. Unlike other saints, whose remains have often served as conduits of divine grace, Mary's body itself was spared from corruption, highlighting her singular purity and close association with her son, Jesus Christ.

Theological reflections on the Assumption often emphasize Mary's role as the new Ark of the Covenant. The original Ark, described in the Old Testament, was a sacred chest that held the Ten Commandments, manna, and Aaron's rod, symbolizing God's presence and His covenant with His people. Mary, in bearing Jesus, the Word made flesh, carried within her the fulfillment of the law and the bread of life, making her the new, living Ark. In the Book of Revelation, John describes a vision of a "woman clothed with the sun, with the moon under her feet, and upon her head a crown of twelve stars" (Revelation 12:1). This woman is often interpreted as Mary, reigning gloriously in heaven, signifying the Assumption and her queenship.

Contemplating the Assumption allows the faithful to understand the profound connection between Mary's earthly life and her heavenly destiny. It serves as an affirmation of the resurrection of the body, which

Christians profess in the Nicene Creed. Mary's life, characterized by obedience to God's will, is crowned not by death, but by her being assumed into heaven. This reinforces the belief that those who live in Christ will be raised up on the last day (John 6:40).

Mary's Assumption also holds a patriotic resonance for many Christians, particularly Catholic veterans and patriots who see in her a model of perfect discipleship and unwavering faith. In times of national struggle and personal trial, Mary's Assumption serves as a beacon of hope and assurance of eternal victory. As the Queen of Heaven, her intercession is sought for guidance and strength, reinforcing the bonds between faith and national identity.

Moreover, the Assumption emphasizes the dignity of the human body. In a world often dominated by materialism and the neglect of spiritual values, Mary's bodily assumption into heaven is a reminder of the sanctity and eternal destiny of the human body. This particular focus can inspire veterans and patriots, who may have seen the ravages of war and the disregard for human life, to revere the body as a temple of the Holy Spirit (1 Corinthians 6:19).

For priests and theologians, the Assumption of Mary is a profound mystery, inviting deeper theological inquiry and teaching. It underscores the unique role of Mary in the economy of salvation and offers a rich vein of reflection on themes such as grace, redemption, and eschatology. Theologians like Saint John Damascene have eloquently articulated the theological significance of the Assumption, affirming that Mary's passage into heavenly glory is a testament to God's loving redemptive plan for humanity.

Philosophers might find in the dogma of the Assumption a profound statement about the human condition and destiny. The belief that a human being, through divine grace, could be taken wholly into the presence of God, challenges naturalist and materialist perspectives, opening avenues for discussions on the intersection of faith and reason, and the metaphysics of personhood and eschatological fulfillment.

As we meditate on the Assumption, we are called to a deeper love for Mary and a firm hope in our own resurrection. Mary's Assumption directs our gaze heavenward and encourages us to live in righteousness and fidelity to God's commandments. It serves as a promise that following Christ will lead to our ultimate glorification, as we partake in the divine nature (2 Peter 1:4).

The Feast of the Assumption, celebrated on August 15, invites Catholics worldwide to reflect on this glorious mystery with renewed devotion and piety. It is a day to celebrate and honor the Mother of God, to contemplate her divine privileges, and to seek her powerful intercession. As we celebrate the Assumption, let us draw inspiration from Mary's life of humility and faith, striving to emulate her virtues to attain the glory that she now enjoys.

In conclusion, the Assumption of Mary is a glorious affirmation of God's salvific work and His plan for humanity. For Roman Catholics, Knights of Columbus, veterans, priests, theologians, and patriots, it is a source of profound hope and inspiration. It reminds us that our earthly pilgrimage, marked by faith and devotion, will ultimately be rewarded with eternal life in the presence of God. As we continue our meditation on "The Glorious Mysteries," let the Assumption of Mary invigorate our hearts with the joy and anticipation of our resurrection, and inspire us to live lives marked by the virtues of our Blessed Mother.

## Thoughts on the Coronation of Mary

The Coronation of Mary, the crowning moment in the Glorious Mysteries, embodies the ultimate exaltation of our Blessed Mother. As Catholics, we see this final mystery not merely as an honor bestowed upon Mary but also as a recognition of her singular role in salvation history. Crowned as Queen of Heaven and Earth, Mary completes the celestial path begun with her Immaculate Conception. In her Coronation, she takes her place beside her Son, Jesus, reigning eternally.

Scripture does not explicitly describe Mary's Coronation, yet Revelation 12:1 offers a profound vision: "And there appeared a great wonder in heaven; a woman clothed with the sun, and the moon under her feet, and upon her head a crown of twelve stars" (Rev. 12:1). The symbolism aligns seamlessly with the Church's dogmatic understanding of Mary's glorification. Cloaked in celestial glory, her reign is pure grace. This exaltation reflects not just her unique role as Theotokos, the Mother of God, but also her singular obedience to God's plan.

Considering Mary's Coronation calls us to reflect on her virtues—her humility, purity, and unwavering faith.

Unlike earthly queens, Mary's reign is devoid of worldly ambition. Her life was marked by a humble acceptance of God's will, from the Annunciation to her Assumption. Mary's enthronement as Queen emphasizes the reward of eternal life, promised to all who emulate her fidelity and service to God.

In meditating upon Mary's Coronation, we are invited to contemplate the profound relationship between the Mother and the Son. Their bond transcends time, illustrating the perfect model of human cooperation with divine grace. Jesus crowned his mother, affirming her pivotal role in His redemptive mission. As patriots and veterans who understand the significance of loyalty, we see in Mary's Coronation the ultimate acknowledgment of her steadfast allegiance to God's mission for humanity. It's a celestial commendation, one that deeply resonates with the heart of every true believer.

Mary's Coronation is also a source of great hope and inspiration. In a world often scarred by turmoil and suffering, her crowning is a testament to the future glory awaiting the faithful. It reminds us that despite the hardships and trials of life, there is a promised joy and fulfillment in the life to come. As patriots and theologians, we understand that true victory often follows immense struggle; Mary's Coronation is the triumphant crescendo following her earthly sorrows and sacrifices.

The historical resilience of great nations sometimes mirrors Mary's journey. Just as she endured and triumphed, so too do nations that rise from adversity to a place of honor. Her Coronation signifies that triumph is not solely of this world. It is a joy so complete and enduring that it can only come from God, the source of all righteousness and justice. This crowns her life of perfect discipleship and unwavering dedication to the divine will.

Furthermore, Mary's Coronation underlines the grace bestowed upon the Church. As the Mother of the Church, her coronation encourages us to recognize the Church's call to holiness and its ultimate destiny. Veterans and Knights of Columbus, invested in the spiritual and moral battles facing society, can draw strength from Mary's elevation. Her celestial queenship is a clarion call to uphold faith, truth, and justice, values that are intrinsic to both religious conviction and national pride.

Biblically, Mary has been a figure of intercession and maternal care, often depicted as the one who brings our petitions to Christ. In her regal role, she doesn't shed these qualities but elevates them. Consider Solomon's honor towards his mother, Bathsheba: "And the king rose up to meet her, and bowed himself unto her, and sat down on his throne, and caused a seat to be set for the king's mother; and she sat on his right hand" (1 Kings 2:19). If an earthly king so reveres his mother, how much more would Christ honor Mary with a celestial crown?

Mary's Coronation also serves to deepen our devotion to her and encourages us to seek her intercession with greater confidence. As we reflect on her elevated status, we find ourselves more drawn to emulate her virtues and to trust in her mediating presence. Philosophers and theologians among us can delve into the richness of Marian doctrines, understanding that this crowning is not an isolated honor but interwoven in the very fabric of Divine Providence and salvation history.

Mary, crowned in heaven, signifies the completion of God's promise to her, "For he hath regarded the low estate of his handmaiden: for, behold, from henceforth all generations shall call me blessed" (Luke 1:48). Her exaltation is God's way of affirming the value of steadfast faith and humble submission to His will. As servants of truth and defenders of faith, emulating Mary's example offers us a virtuous path amidst life's trials.

In our daily lives, as Knights of Columbus, veterans, or simply faithful Catholics, understanding Mary's Coronation can transform how we face challenges. It imbues us with courage and a profound sense of purpose, reminding us of the sovereign grace that accompanies humble service and unwavering faith. Mary's reign invites us to witness to the transformative power of God's love and to inspire others to seek the same.

In conclusion, the Coronation of Mary encapsulates the Blessed Mother's journey from her humble beginnings to her exalted status as Queen of Heaven. This mystery calls us to deeper faith, resilient hope, and dedicated service. It reaffirms the ultimate victory of everlasting grace over temporal suffering, guiding us towards the heavenly crowns promised to all who faithfully serve God. May we, inspired by Mary's celestial coronation, strive to embody her virtues, seeking the eternal joy that only Christ can bestow.

## Chapter 5: The Franciscan Crown Rosary

The Franciscan Crown Rosary, also known as the Rosary of the Seven Joys of Mary, invites the faithful to meditate upon pivotal moments of joy in the Blessed Virgin's life. This unique devotion, cherished by Franciscans, beautifully complements the traditional Rosary by focusing on the Annunciation, the Visitation, the Nativity, the Adoration of the Magi, the Finding of the Child Jesus in the Temple, the Resurrection, and the Assumption and Coronation of Mary. Each Hail Mary recited is a step closer to understanding the deep, maternal love Mary bears for us, her children, and a beacon guiding us to emulate her faith and humility. As you meditate on these joys, be inspired by Mary's profound trust in God's plan, her unwavering love for Christ, and her endless intercession for humanity. "And Mary said, My soul doth magnify the Lord, and my spirit hath rejoiced in God my Saviour" (Luke 1:46-47).

## Reflections on the Seven Joys of Mary

The Seven Joys of Mary, commemorated in the Franciscan Crown Rosary, offer a profound glimpse into the serene yet triumphant heart of our Blessed Mother. Each joy—from the Annunciation, where Mary's humble "Behold the handmaid of the Lord; be it unto me according to thy word" (Luke 1:38), to her Assumption and Coronation, reflecting her ultimate glorification in the presence of her Son—leads us into a deeper appreciation of her unwavering faith and joyous submission to God's will. In these sacred moments, we are invited to contemplate Mary's journey, which mirrors our own call to embrace God's plan with trust and joy. Her joy at the Visitation, Nativity, the Adoration of the Magi, and the Finding of the Child Jesus in the Temple echo through the ages, calling each of us to find God's joy in all circumstances. The Resurrection and Assumption signify not only her joy but also the hope and promise of eternal life for the faithful. By reflecting on these mysteries, we grow closer to understanding Mary's role in salvation history and are inspired to live out our faith with the same jubilant spirit and trust in God's providence.

**The Annunciation**. In the quaint town of Nazareth, an event unfolded that changed the course of history. A humble maid, Mary, lived her days in simplicity and devotion. One day, as the golden light of afternoon gently streamed through her modest home, the archangel Gabriel appeared before her. Clad in divine splendor, Gabriel conveyed a message that would resonate through the ages: "Hail, thou that art highly favoured, the Lord is with thee: blessed art thou among women" (Luke 1:28). Mary was greatly troubled at his words and wondered what kind of greeting this might be.

Gabriel's words, though filled with blessed promise, were also weighty with divine expectation. The angel said unto her, "Fear not, Mary: for thou hast found favour with God. And, behold, thou shalt conceive in thy womb, and bring forth a son, and shalt call his name JESUS" (Luke 1:30-31). This proclamation echoed the prophets of old, heralding the coming of the Messiah, the Savior. Such a revelation was laden with both divine grace and human responsibility.

Mary, in her youth and purity, might have felt an overwhelming trepidation, yet her response was a testament to her unwavering faith: "Behold the handmaid of the Lord; be it unto me according to thy word" (Luke 1:38). In this humble acquiescence, Mary aligned her will entirely with God's, exemplifying perfect obedience and trust.

This moment, often contemplated in the mysteries of the Rosary, invites us to reflect on our own responses to the divine will. Are we as open and accepting as Mary? Do we, in our daily lives, echo her fiat when faced with paths unknown? Her example is a beacon, guiding us to surrender ourselves trustfully into God's hands, even amidst the uncertainties that life inevitably presents.

This acceptance by Mary was not done in the absence of free will but rather in the fullness of it. The Annunciation calls us to understand that true freedom is found in saying "yes" to God. It is in this submission that we encounter divine liberty, a paradox that challenges the secular notion of freedom.

Moreover, the Annunciation holds a profound patriotic resonance. Mary's assent to bear the Savior of the world can be paralleled with the dedication of patriots and veterans who say "yes" to serve and protect their nations. Just as Mary committed herself to the divine mission, soldiers and defenders commit their lives to a cause greater than themselves. This divine calling to service and sacrifice is a reflection of the ultimate sacrifice that would be made by Jesus Christ, Mary's son, for the salvation of all mankind.

As Catholics, Knights of Columbus, and believers, we are imbued with this spirit of service. The Annunciation is not merely a historical event but an ongoing invitation to embrace God's will with courage and devotion. Each time we meditate on this mystery, we are called to emulate Mary's obedience and fidelity, to reaffirm our own commitment to God, and to serve others selflessly.

The magnitude of the Annunciation also offers immense theological and philosophical depth. The incarnation of Jesus signifies the union of divine and human nature, a mystery that theologians have long pondered. It presents a unique nexus where Heaven meets earth, where eternity intersects with time. God's descent into humanity through Mary's "yes" is an act of divine humility and love that should inspire profound reverence and reflection.

In addition, there is a deeply personal dimension to the Annunciation. Mary's encounter with Gabriel shows us that God's voice can reach anyone, anywhere, at any time. It teaches us the importance of being open to divine communication, of listening intently within the silence of our hearts. In our fast-paced world filled with noise and distractions, the Annunciation reminds us to create space for God to speak to us and to heed His call.

For priests, theologians, and philosophers, the Annunciation offers an abundant source of contemplation. It challenges us to delve deeper into the mystery of the Incarnation and explore its implications for our understanding of God, humanity, and the cosmos. The profound humility of God, choosing to become a child within Mary's womb, speaks volumes about His love and desire for intimacy with His creation.

Moreover, the Annunciation sheds light on the role of Mary in salvation history. Her fiat, her "yes," makes her the New Eve, the mother of all who live in Christ. Theotokos, the God-bearer, is given a pivotal position in the narrative of redemption. This acknowledgement elevates the dignity of womanhood and underscores the vital role of women in God's salvific plan. Mary becomes a model for all women, embodying both strength and gentleness, obedience and initiative.

In contemplating the Annunciation, we cannot overlook the faith and virtue of Mary. Her immaculate heart, free from sin, was prepared from the beginning to receive the divine message. Her purity is not merely an absence of sin but a fullness of grace that allowed her to respond with complete faith and willingness. Her example of holiness is one that all faithful are encouraged to emulate, calling us to a deeper conversion and sanctification in our own lives.

Furthermore, the Annunciation is a moment of profound joy. Gabriel announces the coming of the Savior, and this news is cause for great rejoicing. It is the dawn of our salvation, a light breaking into the world's darkness. The joy of the Annunciation inspires our worship and gratitude, deepening our relationship with Christ and fostering a vibrant, joyful faith.

As we meditate on this mystery, let us also consider how the Incarnation reveals God's proximity to us. He is not a distant deity but one who chooses to enter into our human experience, sharing in our joys and sorrows, our struggles and triumphs. This intimacy challenges us to recognize and respond to God's presence in our daily lives, in the mundane and the miraculous alike.

In our role as witnesses to this sacred event, we are encouraged to share the joy and hope of the Annunciation with others. As Mary received the Word and bore it to the world, so are we called to receive Christ into our hearts and bring Him to others through our actions and words. This evangelizing mission is essential, particularly in a world that often seems disconnected from the divine.

In conclusion, the Annunciation is a profound mystery worthy of our deep meditation and reflection. It calls us to faith, service, and sanctity, guiding us closer to God and inspiring us to live out our divine calling with courage and joy. The reverberations of Mary's fiat echo through time, inviting each of us to say our "yes" to God in the unique circumstances of our lives.

**The Visitation** unfolds with a simple yet profound journey, one that speaks to the very heart of faith, humility, and divine joy. Mary, carrying the Son of God in her womb, sets forth to visit her cousin Elizabeth, who is also pregnant, albeit miraculously, in her advanced age. This moment, rich with spiritual significance and human connection, offers a testament to God's providential care and the reciprocal joy found in humble service and mutual support.

Mary's journey to the hill country, aimed at serving Elizabeth, can also be seen as a pilgrimage of faith. As Saint Luke recounts, "And Mary arose in those days, and went into the hill country with haste, into a city of Juda; And entered into the house of Zacharias, and saluted Elizabeth" (Luke 1:39-40). Her haste was not out of urgency but out of heartfelt eagerness to share in Elizabeth's joy and to offer her assistance. This highlights a crucial aspect of the Visitation: the joy and responsibility in caring for others within the family of faith.

Upon Mary's greeting, the child in Elizabeth's womb leapt for joy, and Elizabeth was filled with the Holy Ghost. She exclaimed in a loud voice, "Blessed art thou among women, and blessed is the fruit of thy womb.

And whence is this to me, that the mother of my Lord should come to me?" (Luke 1:42-43). Elizabeth's proclamation, filled with the Holy Spirit, recognized the divine presence within Mary and exemplified the profound recognition of Jesus even before His birth. This interaction between two faithful women underlines the essence of true, God-centered relationships.

Elizabeth's humble acknowledgment of her unworthiness to receive the mother of the Lord reminds us of the attitude we should hold when approaching God. Like Elizabeth, we too may feel unworthy, but we are called to recognize and embrace God's grace with humility and joy. Mary's response to Elizabeth's exclamation is the Magnificat, a song of praise and prophecy that glorifies God's mighty deeds and His mercy.

Mary's Magnificat, "My soul doth magnify the Lord, And my spirit hath rejoiced in God my Saviour" (Luke 1:46-47), sets a template for devotion and praise. This hymn resonates through the ages, encapsulating the joy and reverence due to God, who exalts the humble and fills the hungry with good things. Her words are a beautiful example of theological insight expressed through poetic devotion, marking a profound moment of biblical literature that calls us to a deeper appreciation of God's work in our lives.

The Visitation is also a powerful representation of the communion of saints. Here we see two women, both chosen for divine purposes, leaning on each other for support. Mary's journey to Elizabeth can be viewed as an embodiment of the theological virtues of faith, hope, and charity. Her faith in God's promise, her hope for the fulfillment of God's word, and her charitable actions towards Elizabeth create a powerful narrative that encourages us to live out these virtues in our own lives.

We are reminded that in every act of charity, every journey to serve another, Christ is present. Mary's visit to Elizabeth was not only an act of familial love but a declaration of the presence of God among His people. It signifies that where Christ's followers go, His presence follows. The Visitation challenges us to be bearers of Christ to others, carrying His love and peace to those we encounter.

Moreover, the Visitation encapsulates the theme of joy in the midst of trials. Both Mary and Elizabeth faced challenging circumstances. Mary, a young virgin, accepted the divine call to bear the Savior with great faith, despite the societal implications. Elizabeth, aged and once barren, welcomed the gift of her child with a heart full of gratitude. Their meeting reinforces that joy, inspired by the Holy Spirit, transcends earthly challenges and radiates God's glory.

This scene, rich with the symbols of divine encounter, also prefigures the joyful proclamation of the Gospel. Just as John the Baptist leapt in his mother's womb, signaling the presence of Christ, we are called to recognize and rejoice in the nearness of our Lord. Each encounter with Christ should stir within us a deep and undeniable joy that cannot be contained, much like it did within the unborn John.

As Knights of Columbus, patriots, veterans, and believers, we draw from the Visitation lessons on humility, service, and the transformative power of divine joy. Reflecting on this mystery encourages us to emulate Mary's humility and Elizabeth's recognition of God's wonders. We're called to visit, support, and bring joy to those around us, especially those within our faith communities. This act of selfless service not only honors God but strengthens the bonds within the body of Christ.

The Visitation isn't merely a historical event; it's a living story meant to inspire our daily lives. Mary's and Elizabeth's mutual support exemplifies the kind of fraternal love called for within the Knights of Columbus and all Christian communities. When we serve one another with the same zeal that Mary had, we mirror the Holy Family's love and hospitality, essential virtues for any devout Catholic and loyal patriot.

In understanding the Visitation, we also gain insight into the depth of Marian devotion. Mary, the Theotokos, becomes an accessible intercessor who understands our human experiences. Her willingness to journey to help Elizabeth demonstrates her enduring care for humanity. Devotion to Mary leads us closer to Christ, teaching us to humbly serve and to rejoice in God's presence.

Thus, "The Visitation" becomes both a spiritual lesson and a call to action. It's a reminder that our faith isn't static; it demands movement—towards God and towards one another. Mary's example encourages us to engage actively in our communities, bringing divine joy and support to those in need, just as she did for Elizabeth.

Let us then embrace the spirit of the Visitation, eager to carry Christ within us and recognize Him in those we encounter. Inspired by Mary's journey, we embark on our own, filled with faith, propelled by hope, and rooted in charity, always ready to sing our own Magnificat in praise of God's wondrous deeds.

**The Nativity** unfolds as a profound tapestry of divine intervention and human simplicity, intricately woven into the fabric of salvation history. It is a scene of breathtaking humility and celestial majesty, a paradox that encapsulates the ineffable mystery of the Incarnation. The very act of God becoming man, being born of the Virgin Mary, reframes our understanding of power and vulnerability, kingship and servitude, juxtaposing the divinity of Christ with His humanity.

On that holy night in Bethlehem, as recorded in the Gospel of Luke, a potent mix of wonder, fear, and awe filled the air. "And so it was, that, while they were there, the days were accomplished that she should be delivered. And she brought forth her firstborn son, and wrapped him in swaddling clothes, and laid him in a manger; because there was no room for them in the inn" (Luke 2:6-7). There, among the animals, in a borrowed stable, the King of Kings came into the world, a striking image of humility and grace.

It's in this humble setting that we see the full depth of God's love for humanity. The Shepherds, among the first to receive the angelic announcement, embody the simple and pure hearts that recognize divine glory. "And the angel said unto them, Fear not: for, behold, I bring you good tidings of great joy, which shall be to all people. For unto you is born this day in the city of David a Saviour, which is Christ the Lord" (Luke 2:10-11).

Consider the shepherds' reaction—fear turned to wonder, then to joy and eagerness. Their encounter with the heavenly host transforms their nightly vigil into a celestial celebration, driving them to Bethlehem to witness the fulfillment of prophecy. They became the first evangelists, spreading the good news of the Savior's birth.

Their story, however, is more than a historical account; it is an invitation for us to approach Christ with the same humility and openness. Catechetically, the Nativity teaches us that God often enters our lives in unassuming and unexpected ways. Our own 'Bethlehems'—the ordinary, obscure corners of our existence—are precisely where Christ seeks to dwell.

This moment in sacred history also calls to mind the prophecy of Isaiah: "For unto us, a child is born, unto us a son is given: and the government shall be upon his shoulder: and his name shall be called Wonderful, Counsellor, The mighty God, The everlasting Father,

The Prince of Peace" (Isa. 9:6). Here lies the theological profundity of the Nativity: the eternal Word made flesh, Emmanuel—God with us—ushering in an era of divine peace and reconciliation.

Mary and Joseph, central figures in this divine narrative, exhibit unparalleled faith and obedience. Mary's 'yes'—her fiat—serves as a perpetual model of discipleship. Her contemplative heart, which "pondered these things" (Luke 2:19), reflects a depth of spiritual insight that continues to inspire theologians and devotees alike. Joseph, the righteous man, underscores the virtues of guardianship and quiet strength, sustaining the Holy Family through unwavering trust in divine providence.

In this contemplation of the Nativity, we are also drawn to the broader paradoxes it represents. Christ's birth in poverty contrasts sharply with His heavenly glory. "For ye know the grace of our Lord Jesus Christ, that, though he was rich, yet for your sakes he became poor, that ye through his poverty might be rich" (2 Cor. 8:9). Such divine condescension underscores God's intimate solidarity with the human condition, providing comfort and hope that transcends earthly suffering.

Furthermore, the presence of the Magi in Matthew's Gospel adds another layer of universal significance to the Nativity. These learned men, representing the Gentiles, embark on a journey guided by a star, seeking the newborn King. Their homage prefigures the global mission of the Church, as it spreads the Gospel to all nations. Their gifts—gold for kingship, frankincense for divinity, myrrh for suffering—symbolize the multifaceted identity of the Christ Child (Matt. 2:1-12).

Patriots and veterans may find in the Nativity a powerful inspiration for service and sacrifice. Christ, the ultimate liberator, exemplifies true leadership and sacrificial love, echoing through the centuries in the noble acts of those dedicated to protecting and serving others. His birth heralds a new kind of kingdom, one marked not by dominion and power, but by humility, service, and love.

For priests and theologians, the Nativity is a perennial source of doctrinal richness and spiritual depth. It encapsulates the mystery of the Incarnation—a central tenet of the faith that invites endless contemplation. Here, God enters into human history in a tangible, profound manner, presenting the theological truth that "the Word was made flesh, and dwelt among us" (John 1:14).

Even as we celebrate the birth of Christ, it's essential to remember the fuller context of His mission: redemption through the Cross. The cradle in Bethlehem is but the first step toward Golgotha, reminding us that the Nativity is integrally connected to the Passion and Resurrection. "For this purpose the Son of God was manifested, that he might destroy the works of the devil" (1 John 3:8).

Thus, the Nativity is not merely a moment in time but a perpetual call to embrace God's transformative love. It beckons us to renew our faith, to see Christ in the "least of these" (Matt. 25:40), and to live out the virtues exemplified by the Holy Family. It's a summons to recognize that, just as Christ was born in humble surroundings, He desires to be born anew in the humble, ordinary moments of our lives.

May this reflection on the Nativity deepen our devotion and embolden our witness, inspiring us to carry the light of Christ into a world longing for the hope and peace that only He can provide. As we meditate on this sacred mystery, let us echo the joyful proclamation of the angels: "Glory to God in the highest, and on earth peace, good will toward men" (Luke 2:14).

**The Adoration of the Magi** unfolds a moment brimming with symbolic significance, where divine mystery meets human reverence. In the great drama of salvation, the visit of the Magi illuminates God's magnanimous invitation to all nations to partake in the salvific mission of Christ. Imagine the scene: the Christ child nestled in his mother's arms, visited not by the elite of Jerusalem but by wise men from the East, bearing gifts befitting a king, a priest, and a martyr— gold, frankincense, and myrrh.

The Gospel of Matthew brings this narrative to life, telling us, "Now when Jesus was born in Bethlehem of Judaea in the days of Herod the king, behold, there came wise men from the east to Jerusalem" (Matt. 2:1). These Magi, learned in the stars and ancient prophecies, journeyed far, driven by a celestial phenomenon they could not ignore. Their mission was not merely an academic inquiry but a spiritual pilgrimage, an act of faith.

Their arrival at the humble dwelling of the Holy Family marked an epoch of spiritual inclusiveness. Unlike the shepherds who were invited by the angels, the Magi followed a star—God led them by a means that resonated with their own wisdom and understanding.

This signifies the universality of Jesus' mission: He is the Lord of all nations, meeting each person where they are.

Consider the gifts they brought. Gold, the most precious metal, symbolized kingship. By offering gold, the Magi acknowledged the sovereignty of the Christ child, affirming what the prophet Isaiah had foretold: "For unto us a child is born, unto us a son is given: and the government shall be upon his shoulder: and his name shall be called Wonderful, Counselor, The mighty God, The everlasting Father, The Prince of Peace" (Isaiah 9:6). Frankincense, an aromatic resin used in priestly duties, symbolized divinity and worship. By this offering, the Magi recognized the divine nature of this Child, entering human history to fulfill the priestly role of offering the ultimate sacrifice. Myrrh, commonly used for embalming, foreshadowed His suffering and death, a prophetic nod to His role as the sacrificial Lamb of God.

Thus, the Adoration of the Magi embodies multiple layers of revelation. It affirms Christ's kingly, priestly, and sacrificial roles, laying the groundwork for our understanding of His ultimate mission—salvation through sacrifice. The Gospel scene is filled with rich theological symbolism and typology that echoes throughout Salvation History.

The Magi's journey also speaks volumes about the spirit of inquiry and the virtue of humility. These were wise men, scholars of their age, yet they embarked on a hazardous journey driven by hope and faith. They did not come to dictate terms or to assert their knowledge. They came to adore, to offer homage. Their humility in the presence of divine mystery speaks to the profound truth that wisdom and faith are not adversaries but collaborators in the quest for truth.

Equally meaningful is the Magi's departure. Matthew tells us that being warned in a dream, "they departed into their own country another way" (Matt. 2:12). Whenever we encounter Christ, we are invited to leave by a different path, transformed and renewed. The encounter with the divine changes our course, taking us away from the ways of sin and leading us into the realm of grace.

In this narrative, the Holy Family also exhibits remarkable openness and hospitality. Mary and Joseph, though aware of the extraordinary nature of their child, humbly accept the homage of these exotic visitors. They are not overwhelmed but are instead serene, knowing that they are part of God's divine plan which is unfolding in mysterious ways. The peaceful acceptance shown by the Holy Family provides a model for us in welcoming God's plan, however unexpected it may be.

Let us not overlook the political undertones woven into the story of the Magi. Their appearance unsettles King Herod and the power structures of Jerusalem. The Messiah's birth threatens worldly dominions built on fear and oppression. In their simplicity and faith, the wise men from the East embody the divine subversion of earthly power, proclaiming a new kind of kingship based not on tyranny but on love and justice. Indeed, "He hath put down the mighty from their seats, and exalted them of low degree" (Luke 1:52).

In reflecting upon the Adoration of the Magi, must we not also consider our own lives? Are we vigilant and attentive to the ways God might be calling us, perhaps in unexpected circumstances or through unlikely messengers? Do we possess the courage to journey into the unknown, prompted by a divine light? And upon encountering Christ, do we have the grace to offer all that we hold dear, recognizing Him as King, Priest, and Savior?

For the Roman Catholic believer, the story of the Magi challenges us to deepen our devotion and to broaden our understanding of God's universal call to salvation. It beckons us to embrace a more profound sense of mission, recognizing that our faith journey is not merely for our own edification but also for the illumination of the world. As Knights of Columbus, veterans, patriots, and priests, we are called to be bearers of light in a darkened world, emulating the Magi in our pursuit of truth and our dedication to service.

The Adoration of the Magi resounds as an anthem of hope and divine generosity. It reminds us that no journey is too arduous when Christ is at its end, and no gift is too humble when offered with a heart full of love. Just as the Magi returned to their own country by another route, we, too, are called to chart new paths in our spiritual lives, guided by the light of Christ and the wisdom of the Holy Spirit.

As we meditate on this divine encounter, let us invoke the intercession of the Magi, those wise seekers who followed a star and found the Light of the World. May their example inspire us to seek Christ with unyielding faith and to offer Him the treasures of our hearts with love and humility. In doing so, we echo the heavenly song, "Glory to God in the highest, and on earth peace, good will toward men" (Luke 2:14). Amen.

**The Finding of the Child Jesus in the Temple** offers us a profound glimpse into the early life of Christ, one filled with divine wisdom and purpose even at such a tender age. This event, recounted in the Gospel of Luke, occurs when Jesus is just twelve years old. As devout Jews, Mary and Joseph annually made the pilgrimage to Jerusalem for the feast of Passover, and on this notable journey, they unknowingly left the city without their son (Luke 2:41-43).

The passage opens a window into the hearts of Mary and Joseph, who must have been frantic with worry upon realizing Jesus was not among the traveling company. For three days, they searched anxiously, a period symbolic of the later three days between Christ's crucifixion and resurrection. Their distress is palpable, capturing the very essence of parental concern. When they finally found Him in the temple, their initial relief was mingled with astonishment. There He sat among the doctors of law, "both hearing them, and asking them questions," and all who heard Him were amazed at His understanding and answers (Luke 2:46-47).

This moment is striking, not merely for its emotional impact on Mary and Joseph, but for what it reveals about Jesus' identity and mission. His response to

Mary's question—"How is it that ye sought me? Wist ye not that I must be about my Father's business?"—is as gentle as it is profound (Luke 2:49). Here, Jesus affirms His divine sonship and His commitment to His Heavenly Father's will, a commitment that would define His entire life and ministry.

For the faithful, the finding of the Child Jesus in the Temple offers a lesson in divine purpose and the call to seek God's wisdom. Jesus' youthful engagement with the teachers of the law encapsulates the essence of wisdom that the Book of Proverbs proclaims: "For the Lord giveth wisdom: out of His mouth cometh knowledge and understanding" (Prov. 2:6). It underscores the principle that true wisdom comes from aligning oneself with God's will and seeking His understanding.

Moreover, this episode highlights the importance of the temple as a place of teaching and spiritual growth. It was in the temple that Jesus, even as a child, engaged deeply with the religious traditions and teachings of His people. For Catholics, the church serves a similar role, providing a sanctuary for worship, learning, and communion with God. We can draw inspiration from Jesus' example by fostering a deep connection with our own places of worship, engaging with the teachings, and participating actively in the life of the Church.

This scene also offers a poignant reflection on the nature of familial relationships and the interplay between earthly and heavenly duties. Mary and Joseph's initial reaction upon finding Jesus is deeply human—one of emotional relief and parental admonishment. Yet, Jesus gently reminds them and us that our ultimate loyalty lies with God. He models a perfect balance of respect for His earthly parents while prioritizing His divine mission. As it says in Ephesians 6:1, "Children, obey your parents in the Lord: for this is right," yet we are also reminded of Matthew 6:33, "But seek ye first the kingdom of God, and His righteousness; and all these things shall be added unto you."

Additionally, this narrative can inspire patriotism and a sense of communal life. Mary and Joseph's journey to Jerusalem was undertaken in the spirit of religious observance and national unity, as they joined fellow Israelites in celebrating Passover. Their devotion to religious pilgrimage demonstrates a commitment to communal worship and the collective memory of their liberation from Egypt. Similarly, Catholics are called to participate in the liturgical life of the Church, which binds us together as the Body of Christ and anchors us in our shared faith and traditions.

In converting nonbelievers and catechizing the faithful, this story reveals the inherent draw of divine wisdom. The doctors of the law in the temple were astounded by Jesus' understanding and His answers. The wisdom of God is compelling and transformative. It calls people to listen, to be amazed, and ultimately, to believe. This episode from Jesus' youth can serve as a powerful entry point for those who are new to the faith, demonstrating that God's wisdom surpasses all human understanding and speaks to every heart, regardless of age or background.

Furthermore, this moment in the temple encapsulates the journey of faith every believer must undertake—a journey that involves seeking, questioning, and ultimately finding God. Mary and Joseph's diligent search for Jesus parallels our own spiritual quests. At times, we may feel as though we have lost sight of Christ, and our spiritual journey may be marked by periods of anxious searching. Yet, this story reassures us that, with perseverance, we will find Him where He has been all along—about His Father's business.

Lastly, *The Finding of the Child Jesus in the Temple* encourages us to meditate on the profound mystery of the Incarnation. Jesus, fully divine and fully human, grows in wisdom and stature even as He challenges the very teachers who were considered custodians of divine law. This mystery is beautifully encapsulated in 1 Timothy 3:16: "And without controversy great is the mystery of godliness: God was manifest in the flesh, justified in the Spirit, seen of angels, preached unto the Gentiles, believed on in the world, received up into glory."

As we reflect on this significant event, let us take to heart the lessons it imparts: the pursuit of divine wisdom, the sanctity of our worship spaces, the balance between familial and divine duties, the power of communal faith expressions, the compelling nature of God's wisdom, the persevering journey of faith, and the awe-inspiring mystery of the Incarnation. Each element draws us deeper into the life of Jesus and calls us to a more fervent love and dedication to God.

**Reflections on the Resurrection**... In the darkest hours of humanity, a light burst forth from the tomb, dispelling the shadows of grief and despair. The Resurrection of Jesus Christ stands as the cornerstone of Christian faith, the triumphant proof that death has been vanquished and eternal life assured. "He is not here: for He is risen, as He said. Come, see the place where the Lord lay" (Matt. 28:6). This angelic proclamation not only renewed the spirits of His disciples but continues to ignite the hearts of the faithful across the ages.

The Resurrection invites us to a profound meditation on the transformative power of Christ's victory over death. As Saint Paul emphatically declares, "If Christ be not risen, then is our preaching vain, and your faith is also vain" (1 Cor. 15:14). The Resurrection is not merely an event in the past but a living reality that permeates our lives, infusing our existence with hope and purpose. We are called to participate in His Resurrection, to rise from sin and embrace our new life in Christ.

Consider Mary Magdalene, who came to the tomb while it was still dark. Her sorrow turned to unspeakable joy when she recognized the risen Lord. "Jesus saith unto her, Mary. She turned herself, and saith unto Him,

Rabboni; which is to say, Master" (John 20:16). This intimate encounter mirrors our own moments of rediscovery when faith reignites in the face of adversity, guiding us to recognize and proclaim the living Christ in our midst.

The Resurrection narratives also remind us of the importance of community. When the disciples were gathered in fear, Jesus appeared to them and said, "Peace be unto you" (John 20:19). His presence among them dispelled their fears and infused them with the Holy Spirit, empowering them to be His witnesses to the ends of the earth. This scene exemplifies the communal nature of faith. We, too, are called to gather, to support one another, and to carry the message of the Resurrection to a world yearning for hope.

Indeed, the empty tomb stands as a testament to God's unfathomable love and His divine promise. In the words of the prophet Hosea, "I will ransom them from the power of the grave; I will redeem them from death: O death, I will be thy plagues; O grave, I will be thy destruction" (Hos. 13:14). This promise is fulfilled in Christ, who conquered the grave, offering us the assurance of eternal life.

The Resurrection invites us to rise above our fears and uncertainties, to live boldly as children of the light. It encourages us to seek out the risen Christ in our daily lives, in the sacraments, and in the faces of those we encounter. It also beckons us to transform our world, to be agents of His peace and love, reflecting the radiant light of the Resurrection in all we say and do.

As Knights of Columbus, we are particularly called to embody the spirit of the Resurrection. Our commitment to charity, unity, and fraternity reflects the new life Christ offers. We are to be beacons of hope, supporting our communities and standing up for the downtrodden, echoing the courage of the apostles who, filled with the Holy Spirit, proclaimed the risen Lord without fear.

Moreover, the Resurrection is a call to personal renewal. It challenges us to examine our own lives, to identify the ways we need to die to sin and rise with Christ. This process of conversion is lifelong, as we continually strive to align our lives with the Gospel. We find strength in the words of Saint Paul: "Therefore if any man be in Christ, he is a new creature: old things are passed away; behold, all things are become new" (2 Cor. 5:17).

This transformative power of the Resurrection is beautifully illustrated in the lives of the saints. Consider Saint Francis of Assisi, whose life of radical poverty and humility bore witness to the joy of living for Christ alone. Or Saint Teresa of Avila, whose mystical experiences and reforming zeal were deeply rooted in her intimate relationship with the risen Lord. Their examples inspire us to seek holiness, knowing that through our own small deaths and resurrections, we participate in the victory of Christ.

For veterans and patriots, the Resurrection offers a powerful message of hope and renewal. It assures us that no sacrifice is in vain, that every act of courage and service reflects the ultimate sacrifice of Christ. As we remember our fallen heroes, let us do so with the conviction that death is not the end, but a passage to a new and glorious life. "For if we believe that Jesus died and rose again, even so them also which sleep in Jesus will God bring with Him" (1 Thess. 4:14).

The Resurrection also speaks to us as a nation. In times of division and uncertainty, it calls us to unity and peace, reminding us that our true homeland is not of this world. We are pilgrims, journeying towards the heavenly Kingdom, and our earthly duties are to reflect the justice, mercy, and love of the risen Christ. Let us therefore strive to build a society that upholds the dignity of every person, recognizing in each one the image of our risen Lord.

Priests and theologians, you have a unique role in proclaiming the Resurrection. Through your preaching, teaching, and pastoral care, you bring the message of Easter to life. You are called to help the faithful understand the profound implications of the Resurrection, to guide them in their journey of faith, and to be witnesses of the new life in Christ. Your ministry is vital, as you nourish the Church with the Word and Sacraments, making the risen Lord present in every celebration of the Eucharist.

In conclusion, the Resurrection of Jesus Christ is the heart of our faith, the source of our hope, and the power that transforms our lives. It is a call to rise, to live in the light of Christ, and to proclaim His victory to the world. Let us hold fast to this glorious truth, letting it guide our lives and shape our actions, as we journey towards the eternal Easter, where we will share fully in the joy and glory of the risen Lord. "Thanks be to God, which giveth us the victory through our Lord Jesus Christ" (1 Cor. 15:57).

**The Assumption and Coronation of Mary** ... The Glorious Mysteries invite us into the sublime culmination of the Virgin Mary's earthly journey, marked by the events of her Assumption and Coronation. These mysteries beg us to contemplate the Virgin's singular participation in her Son's Resurrection and Ascension, as well as her exaltation as Queen of Heaven and Earth.

According to Roman Catholic tradition, the Assumption of Mary holds that at the end of her earthly life, the Blessed Virgin was taken up body and soul into heavenly glory. This dogma was solemnly defined by Pope Pius XII in 1950 in the apostolic constitution Munificentissimus Deus. The precise details of Mary's Assumption aren't explicitly recounted in Scripture, but its theological implications ripple through the Bible. In the Old Testament, the Assumption is prefigured in the taking up of Enoch and Elijah (Gen. 5:24; 2 Kings 2:11), while in the New Testament, Mary's role is illuminated through the lens of her participation in her Son's redemptive work.

The Assumption represents a completion of the sanctifying grace bestowed upon Mary from the moment of her Immaculate Conception. Luke's Gospel offers a glimpse of her grace-filled life when the angel Gabriel greets her as "highly favoured" (Luke 1:28), indicating an extraordinary divine favor. This grace culminates in her Assumption, making her the first to share fully in Christ's victory over sin and death. The Assumption, therefore, testifies to the hope that we, too, as members of Christ's body, will one day share in this resurrection.

Reflecting on this mystery, one cannot overlook the joy and veneration with which the early Christians believed in Mary's Assumption. The Church Fathers, such as St. John Damascene and St. Gregory of Tours, echoed this veneration, seeing Mary's Assumption as fitting in the divine economy. St. John Damascene poetically reflected: "It was fitting that she, who had kept her virginity intact in childbirth, should keep her body free from all corruption even after death. It was fitting that she, who had carried the Creator as a child at her breast, should dwell in the divine tabernacles."

Following her Assumption, Mary's Coronation as Queen of Heaven and Earth signifies her unique role in the kingdom of her Son. Though the Book of Revelation provides a symbolic imagery of this event, where "a woman clothed with the sun, and the moon under her feet, and upon her head a crown of twelve stars" (Rev.

12:1), Mary's Queenship is rooted in her divine motherhood and her cooperation in the work of Redemption. Her Coronation epitomizes her intercessory role and her participation in Christ's sovereignty.

This celestial honor bestowed on Mary isn't merely symbolic. It invites us to recognize her maternal care for the Church and her role as a powerful intercessor. Theologians like St. Alphonsus Liguori have emphasized that just as Jesus ascended into heaven to prepare a place for us (John 14:2-3), He also elevated His mother, crowning her as the Queen, to intercede for humanity with a heart full of maternal tenderness.

The tradition of the Coronation of Mary calls to mind the Old Testament tradition of the gebirah, or the queen mother, honored in the Davidic line. Solomon, the son of David, elevated his mother Bathsheba by placing her in a seat of honor (1 Kings 2:19). This ancient tradition finds its fulfillment in Mary, the mother of the eternal King, Jesus Christ. By crowning Mary as the Queen of Heaven, God exalts her humility and her perfect obedience, further accentuating the inextricable link between Mary's life and the Mystery of Salvation.

In times of trial and peril, the faithful have often invoked Mary under her queenly titles, seeking her protection and guidance. The saints and mystics have experienced and attested to Mary's powerful intercession. St. Bernard of Clairvaux cultivated a deep devotion to Mary, famously expressing: "In dangers, in difficulties, in doubts, think of Mary, call upon Mary. Let her name be ever on your lips, ever in your heart; and the better to obtain the help of her prayers, imitate the example of her life."

For modern Catholics, the Assumption and Coronation of Mary serve as profound anchors of hope and faith. They assure us that the final word over our lives belongs not to death but to God's glory and eternal life. By contemplating these mysteries, Catholics are beckoned into a deeper relationship with Mary, who stands as a testament to what God's grace can accomplish. The role model we find in Mary inspires us to live lives rooted in humility, service, and unwavering faith.

The beauty of these mysteries is also found in the communal aspect of their celebration. The feast of the Assumption on August 15 and the Queenship of Mary on August 22 are significant liturgical moments that gather the faithful, uniting them in prayer and reflection. These celebrations reinforce the communal nature of salvation and the Church's shared journey towards eternal life.

Moreover, these mysteries have significant implications for our understanding of the dignity of the human body. The Assumption of Mary emphasizes that our bodies are temples of the Holy Spirit (1 Cor. 6:19-20) and destined for glorification. This understanding challenges us to respect and honor our bodies and those of others, recognizing in them the sacred imprint of the Creator.

As Knights of Columbus, veterans, patriots, and defenders of faith and country, the Assumption and Coronation of Mary call forth a spirit of courage and dedication. These mysteries inspire us to protect the sanctity of life, uphold the dignity of every person, and work towards a society that reflects the values of the kingdom of heaven. The Queen of Heaven, our intercessor and protector, leads us in this noble mission.

Finally, the Assumption and Coronation of Mary offer an invitation to theological reflection and deeper understanding. Priests, theologians, and philosophers are encouraged to delve into the rich theological and ecclesiological significance of these mysteries. In doing so, they unfold the layers of God's salvific plan, revealing the tremendous love and mercy He extends to humanity through the humble handmaid of the Lord.

In conclusion, the Assumption and Coronation of Mary are profound mysteries that illuminate the Church's journey towards eternal glory. They remind us of the powerful intercession of our Heavenly Queen, inspire us to live lives of holiness and service, and fortify us with hope of our own resurrection and eternal life with Christ. As we meditate on these mysteries, may we draw closer to Mary, our Mother and Queen, who leads us ever more deeply into the heart of her Son.

## Chapter 6: The Seven Sorrows Servite Rosary

In the profound reverence of the Seven Sorrows Servite Rosary, we find a pathway that leads us deeper into the compassionate heart of Mary, our Sorrowful Mother. This rosary, distinct in its focus, invites us to meditate on the seven key sorrows that pierced her immaculate heart, starting from the prophecy of Simeon and culminating in the burial of Jesus. "Yea, a sword shall pierce through thy own soul also," foretold Simeon, revealing the intimate suffering Mary would endure (Luke 2:35). Each sorrow offers a unique contemplation on the depth of her love and the immense sacrifice involved in her role as the Mother of God. As we journey through these meditations, we draw strength from Mary's steadfast faith and find solace in her unparalleled example of grace amidst suffering. This sacred devotion not only fortifies our own spiritual resolve but also brings us closer to the redemptive agony of Christ, inspiring us to embrace our crosses with renewed courage and unwavering faith.

## Reflections on the Prophecy of Simeon

The Prophecy of Simeon, found in the Gospel of Luke, marks the first of the Seven Sorrows of Mary. This moment is a profound intersection of joy and heartache, a bittersweet revelation that underscores the gravity of Christ's mission and the immense suffering Mary would endure. "And Simeon blessed them, and said unto Mary his mother, Behold, this child is set for the fall and rising again of many in Israel; and for a sign which shall be spoken against; (Yea, a sword shall pierce through thy own soul also,) that the thoughts of many hearts may be revealed" (Luke 2:34-35).

Simeon's words are a poignant reminder that the life of Christ, though filled with divine purpose, is also steeped in suffering and sacrifice. For Mary, this prophecy transforms the joy of presenting her newborn Son at the Temple into a prelude of impending pain. At this moment, she begins to comprehend the scope of her role as the Mother of Sorrows, chosen by God not only to bring the Savior into the world but also to partake in His suffering.

In this prophecy, Simeon alludes to the division Christ will cause, a division not born out of mere disagreement but one that penetrates the very core of human existence—"for the fall and rising again of many in Israel." The imagery of the sword piercing Mary's soul is a vivid foretelling of the depth of her participation in Christ's redemptive suffering. This prophecy invites believers to reflect on how the divine plan often intertwines joy with sorrow, calling the faithful to accept both as part of God's salvific design.

For Roman Catholics, Knights of Columbus, veterans, and all who hold their faith close, this moment serves as an invitation to emulate Mary's steadfastness. Despite knowing the pain that lay ahead, Mary embraced her calling without hesitation. Her example offers a powerful lesson in courage and faithfulness, virtues that are especially resonant in the lives of those who serve and protect their communities and nations.

It's essential to meditate on Simeon's prophecy with empathy, recognizing the profound emotional and spiritual impact it had on Mary. She had just given birth to the Savior, and the joy of this miraculous event was inseparably linked to the foreseen anguish of His Passion. Mary's acceptance of this dual reality underscores her unparalleled faith and unwavering trust in God's plan, even when faced with unimaginable suffering.

Patriots and veterans may find a parallel in their experiences, where moments of triumph are often shadowed by the burdens of sacrifice. The prophecy of Simeon teaches that bearing these burdens with grace can be a powerful testament to one's faith and commitment to a higher cause. Like Mary, who stood resolutely at the foot of the Cross, those who serve are called to bear witness to their faith through both victories and trials.

Furthermore, this prophecy challenges theologians and philosophers to delve deeper into the paradox of suffering and redemption. Simeon's words provoke thought and discussion on how suffering serves a redemptive purpose within the Christian narrative. This reflection opens up avenues for understanding how personal trials can bring about spiritual growth and a closer union with Christ's suffering.

Priests, in their pastoral care, can draw upon Simeon's prophecy to offer comfort and guidance to their congregations. It presents a way to help parishioners navigate their own sorrows by encouraging them to look to Mary's example. Her ability to accept her sufferings with grace and trust in God's plan can inspire the faithful to find strength and hope amidst their own tribulations.

The prophecy also holds a significant place in catechesis, aiding in the formation of the faithful. It calls for a deepened understanding of the nature of Christ's mission and the essential role of suffering in the Christian life. Educating the faithful about this prophecy can enhance their appreciation of Mary's sorrows and deepen their empathy and connection to her maternal heart.

Simeon's prophecy, when meditated upon within the context of the Seven Sorrows Servite Rosary, enriches one's spiritual journey. It serves as a cornerstone for understanding the intertwining of joy and suffering in the Christian life. By reflecting on this prophecy, the faithful are invited to enter into a more profound empathy with Mary's sorrows, ultimately drawing them closer to Christ.

In conclusion, the Prophecy of Simeon stands as a powerful testament to the complexity and depth of the Christian faith. It beckons believers to embrace their individual crosses with the same courage and faith demonstrated by Mary. Through her example, all faithful are reminded that suffering, when united with Christ, brings forth redemption and eternal glory. The prophecy is a call to embody empathy, strength, and unwavering faith, firmly rooting one's devotion in the trust that God's plan, though mysterious, is always rooted in love and ultimate good.

## Meditations on the Flight into Egypt

The journey to Egypt wasn't just a physical escape; it was a profound testament to God's providence and a vivid illustration of faith under duress. Imagine the Holy Family, thrust from their familiar surroundings into a foreign land, their hearts heavy with uncertainty, yet buoyed by unwavering trust in divine guidance. The flight into Egypt is a reflection of our own spiritual pilgrimages, where faith compels us to move forward, even when the path is unknown.

Joseph's dream, where an angel warned him to flee, embodies the direct intervention of God in human affairs. "And when they were departed, behold, the angel of the Lord appeareth to Joseph in a dream, saying, Arise, and take the young child and his mother, and flee into Egypt, and be thou there until I bring thee word: for Herod will seek the young child to destroy him" (Matt. 2:13). This divine warning illuminates the Shepherd's protective nature over His flock. Joseph's immediate obedience, his silent yet profound yes, is a model of patriarchal sacrifice and fortitude.

The trek to Egypt wasn't a trek of a few miles. It spanned hundreds of miles, fraught with harsh landscapes and potential threats. Yet, through the grit of Joseph, the purity of Mary, and the divine presence of Jesus, we witness the embodiment of holy perseverance. Consider how their journey mirrors our struggles against the trials of life. Each step they took is a testament to overcoming fear with faith, an act of hope in the face of formidable challenges.

Amidst their journey, the Holy Family's reliance on God was absolute. Just as God guided the Israelites through the desert, He guided Joseph, Mary, and Jesus through their own wilderness. "Thy word is a lamp unto my feet, and a light unto my path" (Ps. 119:105). This Scripture rings true as a divine compass, leading them to a place of refuge. Egypt, once a land of bondage for the Israelite ancestors, now became their sanctuary. The irony here is a powerful reminder of God's redemptive plan in all seasons.

Mary's experience during the flight is particularly poignant. As Mother, she carried the weight of anxiety for her child's safety. Her maternal heart bore the sorrow of displacement and the foreboding dangers. Yet, she remained the epitome of grace and trust in God's will. Her suffering prefigures the sorrows she would endure at the foot of the cross. In this trial, she intercedes for all mothers who bear the burden of protection and provision for their families under dire circumstances.

The Flight into Egypt also speaks to the plight of the refugee and the displaced. Jesus, in His infancy, became a refugee, identifying with all who are forced to flee their homes due to violence and oppression. As He later proclaimed, "Inasmuch as ye have done it unto one of the least of these my brethren, ye have done it unto me" (Matt. 25:40). The Holy Family's journey invites us to open our hearts to the stranger and extend our hands to the needy, recognizing Christ in their suffering.

As Church Militant, inspired by the Knights of Columbus' principles of charity, unity, and fraternity, we draw strength from the Holy Family's flight, urging each member to defend the sanctity of family and uphold the dignity of human life. This biblical event is not just a historical account but a living call to embody sacrificial love and unwavering faith amidst modern adversities.

Moreover, the Flight into Egypt demonstrates God's sovereignty over history. Herod's plans to kill Jesus failed, proving that human malice cannot thwart divine providence. "The Lord knoweth the thoughts of man, that they are vanity" (Ps. 94:11). This assures us that, despite the turmoil and treachery of the world, God's plans for salvation and redemption will always prevail. We are called to trust in His sovereignty, especially when the world's chaos seems overwhelming.

For our veteran brothers and sisters, the journey of the Holy Family can be seen as a parallel to the battles fought for freedom and protection. The call to arms, the response to duty, and the sacrifices made echo Joseph's silent acceptance of his role as protector and provider. The strength and resilience required for such arduous tasks are inspired by divine grace. Reflecting on the Flight into Egypt can provide spiritual fortitude amidst the service's physical and emotional challenges.

The theologians and philosophers among us may find in the Flight into Egypt a wealth of insights into the nature of divine direction and human response. It's a profound commentary on free will met with divine foreknowledge. God's plans do not negate human action but invite it into a mysterious collaboration where faith and deeds work harmoniously. This mystery leads us deeper into contemplation of God's omniscience and omnipresence.

As we meditate on the Flight into Egypt, let it deepen our resolve to live out our vocations with Joseph's obedience, Mary's faith, and Jesus' humility. Every challenge met with faith becomes a pilgrimage toward divine intimacy. Let us carry this story in our hearts, remembering that God's guiding hand is always upon us, leading us out of danger and into His everlasting light.

## Contemplations on the Loss of the Child Jesus in the Temple

In the journey of life, the moments of loss and bewilderment we encounter often mirror the sorrow that the Blessed Virgin Mary and Saint Joseph felt when they discovered the absence of their beloved Child, Jesus. The account of this profound event illuminates both the human experience of anxiety and the divine mystery of Christ's mission. Here, we delve into this poignant episode, not merely as a historical event, but as a profound lesson in faith, trust, and divine wisdom. This contemplation serves as the third sorrow in the Seven Sorrows Servite Rosary, inviting us to meditate deeply on the spiritual truths and emotional depths contained in that experience.

The Holy Family traveled to Jerusalem for the Feast of Passover, fulfilling their religious obligations with joy and devotion (Luke 2:41). After the feast, Mary and Joseph departed, believing Jesus to be among their kinfolk. It was not until they journeyed a day's distance that they realized He was missing. Their hearts must have trembled with concern as they retraced their steps back to the Holy City, searching frantically amidst the throngs of pilgrims. This intense period of searching—

three days long—culminates in their finding Jesus in the Temple, engaged in deep discussion with the teachers, listening and asking profound questions (Luke 2:46).

The pain of separation and the anxiety of not knowing the whereabouts of their Child bring to light the very essence of human anguish and parental concern. The initial reaction of Mary encapsulates this maternal sorrow as she exclaims: "Son, why hast thou thus dealt with us? behold, thy father and I have sought thee sorrowing" (Luke 2:48). Her words reflect a mother's heart, torn between the reverence for her Child's wisdom and the very human concern for His safety. This duality of emotions—divine reverence and human anxiety—serves as a mirror to our own lives, wherein faith must often coexist with incomprehension and distress.

Jesus' response, though initially perplexing, opens a window into the divine nature of His mission: "How is it that ye sought me? wist ye not that I must be about my Father's business?" (Luke 2:49). Here lies a profound moment of revelation. Christ emphasizes His divine filiation and the ultimate purpose of His presence on earth. His mission transcended the immediate comprehension of even His nearest kin. In this way, the sorrow of losing Him extends into a deeper call for trust in the divine plan, even when it surpasses human understanding.

As we contemplate this scene, we are invited to reflect on the times we have felt bereft of divine presence, moments where we seem to search in vain for answers. The Holy Family's ordeal teaches us that faith persists even in absence. Their distress and subsequent relief upon finding Jesus is a metaphor for our spiritual journey—marked by periods of separation and reunion with the Divine.

Mary's role in this episode is particularly enlightening. Despite her initial confusion, her faith remains unshaken. Standing as the Mother of Sorrows, she offers us a model of persevering faith amidst trials. Her example encourages us to maintain our devotion and trust in God, even when we do not fully grasp His workings. It calls to mind the Scripture: "Trust in the Lord with all thine heart; and lean not unto thine own understanding. In all thy ways acknowledge him, and he shall direct thy paths" (Prov. 3:5-6).

The emotional and spiritual dimensions of this sorrow are multifaceted. It stresses the importance of patience and perseverance in our faith journey. The initial panic and subsequent calm that Mary and Joseph experience remind us that divine consolation follows human tribulation. This sorrow challenges us to find Jesus intentionally and to recognize His presence in our everyday lives, especially in our times of distress.

We must also ponder deeply the significance of the Temple as the setting for this sorrowful mystery. The Temple, being the heart of Jewish worship and the dwelling place of God's presence, symbolizes the ultimate unity between God and humanity. Jesus' presence in the Temple foreshadows the new covenant He will establish. It is here that the transient loss becomes an eternal finding, shedding light on the fulfillment of His mission—reconciling humanity with the Divine. This act echoes the promise: "The Lord is nigh unto all them that call upon him, to all that call upon him in truth" (Ps. 145:18).

In our personal reflections, let us ask for the intercession of the Blessed Virgin Mary, who understands the depths of a parent's worry and the peaks of spiritual revelation. May her example inspire us to trust in God's purpose, even when we find ourselves walking through the valley of uncertainty. As we pray through this sorrowful mystery, let us offer our moments of bewilderment and loss to the Lord, asking Him to grant us the grace to find Him anew, just as Mary and Joseph did.

This contemplation calls us to a deeper understanding of the intricate relationship between human experience and divine will. It beckons us to recognize that in our most heart-wrenching searches, God remains steadfast at work, shaping our faith and drawing us closer to His infinite love and wisdom.

## Insights on the Meeting of Jesus and Mary on the Way of the Cross

As Jesus carried the cross to Golgotha, He encountered not just the jeering crowds, but also a profound, heart-wrenching moment with His Blessed Mother, Mary. This moment holds its own unique sorrow, one which encapsulates the emotional and spiritual agony shared between a mother and her son. When Christ stumbled under the weight of the cross, Mary, witnessing His suffering, felt a sword pierce her own soul as foretold by Simeon: "Yea, a sword shall pierce through thy own soul also, that the thoughts of many hearts may be revealed" (Luke 2:35). The beauty of this encounter speaks to the depths of Christ's love for humanity and the unwavering faith and co-suffering of His mother.

This sorrowful meeting is often depicted with Jesus locking eyes with Mary, an exchange that transcends words. In this silent interaction, their mutual suffering connects deeply with the human experience of pain and loss. Jesus' mission to redeem humanity brings Him inevitable agony, but it is through the eyes of Mary that we see the full horror of His sacrifice. They share a poignant moment, one that embodies the ultimate offering of love and obedience to God's will. This eloquent silence reflects what many veterans and patriots understand: the unspeakable cost of duty and sacrifice for a greater cause.

The Scriptures may not provide a detailed narrative of this meeting, yet the Church's sacred tradition and devout imagination fill in the gaps, reminding us of the tender bond between Jesus and Mary. Consider the words of Lamentations, which captures the anguish of a mother witnessing suffering: "Is it nothing to you, all ye that pass by? Behold, and see if there be any sorrow like unto my sorrow, which is done unto me, wherewith the Lord hath afflicted me in the day of His fierce anger" (Lam. 1:12). This verse resonates with the encounter, highlighting the profound affliction Mary endured.

In contemplating this fourth sorrow, one must reflect upon the dual roles Mary holds — as the Mother of God and as the suffering mother of the Suffering Servant. Her unique position in salvation history offers her a deep connection to the anguish of humanity, making her a powerful intercessor and a beacon of hope. For those engaged in theological reflection, Mary's participation in Jesus' Passion provides a profound image of co-redemption, showing that through suffering, love is perfected and redemption is achieved.

The pain Mary experienced on the way to Calvary speaks volumes about the maternal bond and the universal nature of suffering. Roman Catholics, especially those who are parents, can find solace in Mary's fortitude and her unwavering faith. Her presence alongside Jesus, despite the agony, is a testament to her strength and dedication. This maternal figure, unwavering even in the face of immense sorrow, encapsulates the ideals of loyalty and steadfastness that knights and veterans hold dear.

Moreover, the encounter between Jesus and Mary on the Via Dolorosa unveils the very essence of compassion. Compassion, derived from the Latin "compati," means "to suffer with." Mary embodies this as she accompanies Jesus, physically and spiritually sharing in His Passion. This shared suffering teaches us about the power of empathy and the importance of standing beside those who are afflicted, whether they are our compatriots or strangers. It brings to mind the verse from Galatians: "Bear ye one another's burdens, and so fulfill the law of Christ" (Gal. 6:2).

For priests and theologians, the reflection on this sorrow provides rich material for pastoral care. Mary's role emphasizes the importance of presence — the power of simply being with someone in their darkest moments. It speaks to the pastoral mission of the Church to accompany the suffering, to offer spiritual and emotional support, mirroring Mary's quiet strength. Her actions call the faithful to a deeper understanding of mercy and compassion, encouraging them to elevate their own responses to suffering within their communities.

Furthermore, this meeting on the Way of the Cross exemplifies the ultimate submission to God's salvific plan. Mary's acceptance of her role, despite its immense demands and pain, reflects her profound humility and trust in God's divine providence. "And Mary said, Behold the handmaid of the Lord; be it unto me according to thy word" (Luke 1:38). This acceptance, reiterated throughout her life but especially in this moment, shows the depth of her obedience and faith — qualities that all believers are called to emulate.

Reflecting on the meeting of Jesus and Mary on the Way of the Cross also deepens our understanding of the nature of divine love. It portrays a love that is sacrificial and self-giving, echoing St. John's proclamation: "Greater love hath no man than this, that a man lay down his life for his friends" (John 15:13). The mutual sacrifice of Jesus and His mother amplifies this teaching, urging the faithful to embody a love that transcends pain and suffering for the greater good of humanity.

For Mary, this encounter is a moment of bearing the weight of not just her son's cross but the future crosses of all Christians. Her sorrow offers a tangible example of enduring love and the strength found in faith. Her silent witness calls to mind the virtues of patience, resilience, and faith that the Church holds dear. It reassures us that, while suffering is inevitable, it is not without purpose or redemption.

As we meditate on this painful but profoundly intimate moment, we are called to enter into the sorrow, to feel it, and to allow it to transform our hearts. This sorrow teaches compassion, fortitude, and unwavering faith in God's plan. Whether you are a theologian, a veteran, a priest, or a layperson, the encounter between Jesus and Mary on the Way of the Cross serves as a profound reminder of the power of love, sacrifice, and enduring fidelity to God's will. May this reflection inspire us to carry our own crosses with faith, standing in solidarity with those who suffer, and trusting in the ultimate redemption promised through Christ's Passion.

## Thoughts on the Crucifixion and Death of Jesus

The Crucifixion and Death of Jesus stand at the pinnacle of human history and divine intervention. It is the epicenter of the Christian faith, a paradox of both immense sorrow and profound love. The crucifixion was not merely an event in history but a divine necessity, a culmination of God's intricate plan to redeem humanity from sin. For Roman Catholics and indeed all Christians, contemplating the death of Christ calls for deep empathy and reverence, as we seek to understand the immeasurable sacrifice of Jesus' passion.

The Gospels lay bare the agonizing reality of Jesus' final hours. We read in John, "They crucified him, and two other with him, on either side one, and Jesus in the midst" (John 19:18). It is a stark depiction of Jesus amidst malefactors, highlighting His abject humility. Yet, it is in this humility that His kingship is revealed. The crucifixion on Golgotha, 'The Place of the Skull,' becomes the site where the unfathomable love of God meets the deepest suffering of man. Here, Jesus fulfills His role as the Suffering Servant, foretold by Isaiah, who bore our sins and crushed under the weight of our iniquities (Isa. 53:5).

The Crucifixion is an excruciating image to bear, both physically and spiritually. The nails driven into His hands and feet, the crown of thorns pressing into His brow, each step of the way marked by lashes and mocking. Jesus' cry on the cross: "My God, my God, why hast thou forsaken me?" (Mark 15:34), echoes the lamentations of countless souls throughout history, yet it also serves as a call back to the Psalms where faith triumphs over despair. It is a point of convergence where human anguish meets divine trust, showing that even in utter loneliness, God remains present.

In reflecting on Jesus' death, we are called to introspection. How do we respond to such love? His words, "Father, forgive them; for they know not what they do" (Luke 23:34), embody the infinite capacity of divine mercy. Even in His final moments, Jesus exemplifies the ultimate act of forgiveness. This should inspire us toward a life of forgiveness and compassion, challenging us to emulate His boundless love and mercy.

Patriots, veterans, and defenders of freedom often understand sacrifice more profoundly. Yet, no earthly sacrifice can match the divine sacrifice at Calvary. There, Jesus paid the ultimate price for our freedom from sin. Meditating on His crucifixion engenders a deeper understanding of duty, service, and love for neighbor. It kindles within us a sense of gratefulness and a call to live out our lives in service to others, mirroring the selflessness of Christ.

The darkness that covered the earth during Jesus' final hours (Luke 23:44-45) is symbolic of the world's spiritual state without God. The veil of the temple was rent in twain, signifying that the separation between God and man was now obliterated (Matt. 27:51). By His death, Jesus opened the door to eternal life, making the divine accessible to all. The death of Jesus is thus a testament to the boundless possibilities of divine grace.

A profound part of this meditation is recognizing that the crucifixion was not the end. It was, rather, the beginnings of the promise fulfilled. "For if we have been planted together in the likeness of his death, we shall be also in the likeness of his resurrection" (Rom. 6:5). Jesus' death paves the way for the resurrection, a cornerstone of our faith, and offers us hope for our own resurrection and eternal life.

As theologians and philosophers delve deeper into the enormity of the crucifixion, they unravel layers of divine wisdom and love. St. Paul's reflections in his epistles often circle back to the crucifixion as the central theme of Christian theology. "But God commendeth his love toward us, in that, while we were yet sinners, Christ died for us" (Rom. 5:8). This foundational truth urges us to continually return to the cross, to draw our strength, inspiration, and understanding of our faith.

For priests and lay ministers, the crucifixion is the focal point of our liturgical celebrations, particularly the Eucharist. In every Mass, we commemorate Christ's sacrifice, remembering His words at the Last Supper, "This is my body, which is given for you" (Luke 22:19). The Eucharist transforms our meditation into tangible reality, a perpetual reminder of Christ's ongoing presence and sacrifice for us. Each participation in Holy Communion calls us to a deeper appreciation of the crucifixion and challenges us to live Eucharistic lives of self-giving love.

In contemplating the crucifixion, let us remember that Jesus' death is not merely a subject for sorrow but a cause for profound gratitude and hope. His death is the ultimate act of love and the gateway to salvation. Reflecting on this can deepen our faith, encourage conversion for nonbelievers, and inspire a more fervent patriotism by aligning our actions with Christ's example of selfless love and service.

The Seven Sorrows Servite Rosary's meditation on the crucifixion serves as a poignant reminder of our Lord's greatest act of love. Each bead and prayer draws us closer to understanding the gravity and grace of His sacrifice. As we journey through these reflections, may our hearts be ever softened, our spirits uplifted, and our commitment to embodying Christ's love in our world strengthened.

In our daily lives, let this meditation remind us that every cross we bear, every pain we endure, is united with Christ's sacrifice. Jesust apostolic mission bestows dignity upon our suffering. As we carry our crosses, we are not alone. He is with us, transforming our pain into a conduit of grace and a path to sanctification.

Concluding our thoughts, let us embrace the transformative power of Jesus' crucifixion and death. May it inspire us to live lives of courage, mercy, and unwavering faith, committed to sharing the Good News and glorifying God in all we do.

## Reflections on the Body of Jesus Being Taken Down from the Cross

The scene of Jesus' lifeless body being taken down from the cross is one of profound sorrow and deep contemplation. As we meditate on this sorrowful mystery, we are drawn into the heartbreak and profound grief that enveloped Mary, the mother of Jesus, as well as His followers who witnessed this moment. This act, filled with excruciating pain and tender love, invites us to reflect on the very essence of sacrificial love and ultimate redemption.

In the Gospel of John, we read: "After this, Joseph of Arimathaea, being a disciple of Jesus, but secretly for fear of the Jews, besought Pilate that he might take away the body of Jesus: and Pilate gave him leave. He came therefore, and took the body of Jesus" (John 19:38). This passage reveals the courage and devotion of Joseph of Arimathaea, who risked his own safety to ensure a dignified burial for our Lord. The act of lowering Jesus from the cross was not merely an act of removal but a somber, sacred duty carried out with reverence and love.

Each tug and pull to free Jesus' body from the nails must have been agonizing for those involved. The anguish Mary felt as she held her Son, now pale and cold, is beyond what words can capture. This sorrow is echoed in the prophesy spoken to her by Simeon: "Yea, a sword shall pierce through thy own soul also" (Luke 2:35). In this moment, the full realization of her pain comes to fruition, embodying the thorough and profound sorrow of a mother losing her child in such a brutal and public manner.

Our reflections on the Body of Jesus being taken down from the Cross call us to contemplate the human and divine aspects of this act. How could the Redeemer of the world be brought so low, suffering and dying a criminal's death? This paradox lies at the heart of our faith, for in His lowering, in His absolute humility and obedience unto death, He was exalted. Paul's letter to the Philippians states: "And being found in fashion as a man, he humbled himself, and became obedient unto death, even the death of the cross" (Philippians 2:8).

Joseph of Arimathaea and Nicodemus, who accompanied him, display an incredible example of discipleship and bravery. Though they had been secret followers of Jesus, the darkness of His death removed their fear, replacing it with a bold commitment to honor Him. It was through their hands that Jesus' body was prepared and lain in the tomb, fulfilling the scripture: "And he made his grave with the wicked, and with the rich in his death; because he had done no violence, neither was any deceit in his mouth" (Isaiah 53:9).

As believers, this reflection urges us to consider our own acts of devotion and courage. Are we willing to step out in faith, to risk scorn or persecution to honor our Savior? The sacrifice of Christ calls us to a higher level of commitment, one that may demand our time, our resources, and sometimes even our safety or reputation.

Mary's sorrow, too, invites us to delve into the mystery of co-redemptive suffering. Her participation in the salvific act of her Son was not passive. Every wound inflicted upon Jesus was felt deeply in her immaculate heart. Her unwavering faith, her silent endurance, and her heartfelt lamentation offer us a perfect model of sincere devotion and the depth of a mother's love. We can look to Mary as the first and most faithful disciple, who stood by Her Son from the prophecy of His birth to the solemn moment of His death.

The stripping of Jesus from the cross and the placing of His body into the arms of His mother also brings us face to face with human mortality. The physical body of God-incarnate laid in the arms of Mary speaks profoundly about the vulnerability and the sacredness of human life. Psalm 22:14, a prophetic psalm of David, eerily captures this moment: "I am poured out like water, and all my bones are out of joint: my heart is like wax; it is melted in the midst of my bowels." In these words, we see a foreshadowing of Jesus' supreme sacrifice and utter abandonment.

Finally, when we contemplate this scene, we are called to a deeper understanding of the paschal mystery — the suffering, death, and resurrection of Jesus Christ. In these sorrowful moments, seeds of hope are sown. The darkness that covered the land as Jesus took His last breath will give way to the dawn of the resurrection. Thus, the moment of Jesus being removed from the cross is not merely an endpoint but a pivotal transition to the miraculous beginning of redemption and eternal life.

We should strive to internalize this mystery in our daily lives. When faced with our own crosses, remembering that death is not the end but the precursor to new beginnings can be deeply consoling. This reflection implores us to carry our crosses with faith and perseverance, looking toward the resurrection promised to those who believe in Him.

In conclusion, the act of taking Jesus down from the cross is rich with theological, spiritual, and emotional depth. It is a poignant moment that encapsulates the grievous price of sin and the extraordinary love of God. As we meditate on this sorrow, let our hearts be inflamed with a renewed fervor to live out our faith courageously and with a depth of compassion reflective of the agony and love witnessed in this solemn act.

**Meditations on the Burial of Jesus**

The burial of Jesus, a moment draped in deep sorrow and solemn reverence, stands as a profound meditation within the Seven Sorrows Servite Rosary. When we reflect on this event, every detail of the burial invites us to delve into a mystery both devastating and hopeful. The very act of laying Jesus in the tomb signifies the seeming finality of death, yet, in our faith, it also becomes a prelude to the resurrection. This moment is a crucible where the raw materials of human grief, divine promise, and ultimate redemption converge.

The Gospels recount the actions of Joseph of Arimathea, a silent disciple until this crucial moment. His appearance offers a meditation on bravery and devotion. "He went unto Pilate, and begged the body of Jesus. Then Pilate commanded the body to be delivered" (Matt. 27:58). Let us contemplate the courage it took for Joseph to step forward in a politically tumultuous time, risking his own position and safety. His actions embody the finest qualities of discipleship—courage, stewardship, and reverence for the sacred.

In the lifeless form of Jesus, we see an image that compels both sorrow and awe. Mary, His blessed mother, cradles His body with a piercing sorrow that fulfills the prophecy of Simeon: "Yea, a sword shall pierce through thy own soul also" (Luke 2:35). This image calls us to ponder the maternal heart of Mary, who shares uniquely in the sufferings of Jesus. Her sorrow, yet untainted by despair, becomes a powerful intercession for all who suffer. Mary is ever the Compassionate Mother, guiding her children through their own valleys of the shadow of death.

As Joseph and Nicodemus prepare Jesus' body for burial, we are drawn into another layer of the mystery. "And there came also Nicodemus, which at the first came to Jesus by night, and brought a mixture of myrrh and aloes, about an hundred pound weight" (John 19:39). Their meticulous care in anointing and wrapping His body in linen signifies the respect and honor due to the Son of God. This act of preparation is not merely ritual; it is a profound acknowledgment of the sanctity of Jesus' human form, which bore the marks of suffering for our redemption.

The tomb itself is another focal point for meditation. "Now in the place where he was crucified there was a garden; and in the garden a new sepulchre, wherein was never man yet laid" (John 19:41). A newly hewn tomb, a place of physical death, juxtaposed with a garden, a symbol of life and growth, sets the stage for resurrection. This imagery compels us to look beyond apparent endings to the promise of new beginnings in Christ.

The silence of the tomb is profound. Jesus laid in the sepulchre, which Joseph had hewn out in the rock (Matt. 27:60). The stone rolled against the door seals the physical reality of His death, a moment heavy with finality. For the faithful, this silence is a call to trust deeply in God. It is a moment that challenges our faith, prompting us to listen, to wait, and to hope. This sepulchral silence is replete with divine mystery; it is the quiet before the triumphal shout of resurrection morning.

Let us also meditate on the Roman guards placed at the tomb, a detail loaded with irony and divine purpose. "Pilate said unto them, Ye have a watch: go your way, make it as sure as ye can" (Matt. 27:65). Their presence, intended to prevent any disturbance, becomes yet another divine thread woven into the tapestry of redemption. This act of guarding the tomb highlights the futile attempts of human authority to contain the divine, illustrating the almighty power of God over death and human machinations.

When we consider the women who stood by Jesus during His crucifixion and later visited His tomb, our hearts are moved by their fidelity. They came early in the morning, seeking the body of their Lord, embodying the virtues of perseverance, faith, and love. "And Mary Magdalene and the other Mary, sitting over against the sepulchre" (Matt. 27:61). Their vigil at the tomb transforms into a discovery of the empty grave, a pivotal moment that signifies the dawning of a new era in salvation history.

As we reflect on this sorrowful event, we perceive every stone, every tear, and every whisper of prayer, deepens our intimacy with Jesus. The burial is a testament to the profound mystery of Divine Love—God, who would not only take on human flesh but also undergo the utter humbling of death. When contemplating the burial, let's allow it to enrich our understanding of self-sacrifice, underscoring that through Christ's death and burial, we gain life eternal.

This meditation, therefore, calls us to a deeper sense of reverence and gratitude. It reminds us that in every

Good Friday experience of our lives, the seeds of Easter morning are sown. As we lay our sorrows and sins at the tomb of Christ, may we rise with renewed faith and hope, prepared to embrace the fullness of God's promise.

## Chapter 7: The Divine Mercy Chaplet

The Divine Mercy Chaplet is a profound devotion given to us through the revelations to Saint Faustina, emphasizing God's boundless mercy towards every soul. Praying this chaplet, especially at the Hour of Mercy—3 PM, the hour Jesus died on the cross—opens our hearts to receive grace and compassion as we reflect upon Christ's sacrificial love. As the Apostle Paul exhorts us, "By grace are ye saved through faith; and that not of yourselves: it is the gift of God" (Eph. 2:8). True devotion to the Divine Mercy helps to cultivate a deep trust in Jesus, urging us to surrender our fears and failings to His care. In this way, we answer the call to love one another as He has loved us, spreading the message of divine mercy far and wide. Therefore, let us come together in faith, invoking God's mercy upon ourselves and the whole world through this powerful prayer.

## Reflections on the Divine Mercy Image

The Divine Mercy Image, as revealed to Saint Faustina Kowalska, is a profound visual representation of Christ's infinite mercy. This image is not simply a work of art but a theological message incarnate in strokes of paint. It stands as a beacon of hope, inviting the faithful to delve deep into the mystery of divine compassion and love. Painted according to the instructions given by Jesus to Saint Faustina, the image demands contemplation and reflection, serving as a conduit for divine grace and an invitation to trust in God's boundless mercy.

In the image, Christ is portrayed with one hand raised in blessing and the other pointing to His heart, from which emanate two rays of light, one red and the other pale. The red ray symbolizes the blood of Christ, which is the life of souls. It reminds us of the sacrificial love of Jesus, who suffered and died on the cross for our salvation. Scriptural texts echo this profound reality: "But one of the soldiers with a spear pierced his side, and forthwith came there out blood and water" (John 19:34). This verse underscores the depth of Christ's sacrificial love, a love that is continually offered to humanity.

The pale ray, on the other hand, represents the water that cleanses and purifies souls. It is an invitation to immerse oneself in the sacrament of Baptism and Penance, through which we receive new life and forgiveness. "He that believeth and is baptized shall be saved" (Mark 16:16), highlighting the transformative power of divine mercy channeled through the sacraments. These sacraments are the lifelines for every Christian, renewing and strengthening our bond with the Almighty.

The posture of Christ in the Divine Mercy Image, with His calm yet piercing gaze, communicates an abundance of peace and serenity. This aspect of the image calls upon each of us to approach Jesus with trust and surrender, believing that His mercy is greater than any sin or weakness. The inscription at the bottom, "Jesus, I trust in You," is both a prayer and a proclamation of faith. It invites believers to abandon their fears, doubts, and anxieties at the feet of Jesus, embracing the peace only He can offer.

Trust is a central theme in the Divine Mercy devotion. The image serves as a visual reminder of Christ's promise to those who place their trust in Him. "Come unto me, all ye that labour and are heavy laden, and I will give you rest" (Matt. 11:28). This call extends to every burdened heart, offering solace and rest in the loving embrace of Jesus. The rays emanating from His heart are not merely artistic embellishments but real, enduring symbols of His ever-present grace and mercy.

Reflecting on the Divine Mercy Image also invites us to consider our response to this divine gift. The mandate given to Saint Faustina was clear: act as an apostle of mercy, sharing this message with the world. Each contemplation upon this image beckons a personal commitment to live out the Gospel of mercy in our daily lives. We are called to be merciful as our Heavenly Father is merciful, engaging in acts of compassion, forgiveness, and love.

When priests, theologians, and lay faithful meditate on this image, there lies a deeper theological exploration into the nature of God's mercy. It is a mercy that is not passive but actively seeks out the sinner, urging conversion and renewal. "The Lord is merciful and gracious, slow to anger, and plenteous in mercy" (Psalm 103:8). This verse reflects the patience and enduring kindness of God, an invitation to return to Him regardless of our past.

Moreover, the image presents a Christ who is both divine and human, radiating divine mercy while embodying the frailty of human suffering. His wounds are visible, reminding us of His sacrifice, yet His posture is one of invitation and openness. This duality is crucial for understanding the Incarnation – that God became man to save humanity through His love and mercy. "And the Word was made flesh, and dwelt among us" (John 1:14). This mystery of the Incarnation is at the heart of the Divine Mercy devotion.

For veterans and patriots, the image of Divine Mercy may resonate deeply, offering solace and hope amid the scars of war and conflict. It serves as a reminder that no matter the wounds inflicted by life, Christ's mercy can heal and restore. The rays of mercy can penetrate even the darkest moments, bringing light and peace. The struggles and sacrifices made for the nation can find their true meaning when enveloped in Christ's merciful love.

Theologians and philosophers can engage with the image to explore the profound truths it encapsulates. The Divine Mercy Image becomes a thesis on God's interaction with humanity, extending beyond mere symbolism into the lived experience of grace. It challenges intellectual pursuit to marry with personal transformation, merging the head with the heart.

Contemplating the Divine Mercy Image also fosters a deeper appreciation of the Eucharist. The blood and water flowing from Christ's heart during the Crucifixion point to the sacraments of the Eucharist and Baptism. "This is my blood of the new testament, which is shed for many for the remission of sins" (Matt. 26:28). The Eucharist, as the source and summit of Christian life, is a continuous gift of Jesus' mercy, given to nourish and sustain.

Priests are particularly called to propagate the message of Divine Mercy. In their pastoral mission, the image can be a powerful tool to draw people to the sacrament of Reconciliation. The image standing in the confessional can be an invitation for the penitent to trust in God's forgiveness. Preaching on this image can reignite the flame of faith and hope in the hearts of the faithful, leading them closer to the heart of Jesus.

Ultimately, the Divine Mercy Image is more than an artifact; it is a living encounter with Jesus Christ. Each time we gaze upon it, we are reminded of the infinite love and mercy that emanate from His Sacred Heart.

For every Knight of Columbus, every theologian, every lay faithful, this image is a call to action – to trust deeply, to live mercifully, and to proclaim boldly the mercy of God.

In closing, reflecting on the Divine Mercy Image draws us into the depths of God's love, beckoning us to experience His mercy anew. We are reminded that no sin is too great to be forgiven, no distance too far to be bridged by His love. As we continue to meditate on this profound visual representation, may we allow its message to transform our hearts and lives, responding with trust and extending mercy to others. Let the words "Jesus, I trust in You" be inscribed not just on the image, but on our hearts and tongues, guiding us in our journey of faith.

## Meditations on Trusting in Jesus

Trusting in Jesus is a profound journey of the heart, mind, and soul. It requires an unwavering confidence in His love and mercy, a conviction that sustains us through trials and tribulations. This trust is the cornerstone of the Divine Mercy Chaplet, as it teaches us to surrender our lives into His merciful embrace. "Trust in the Lord with all thine heart; and lean not unto thine own understanding" (Prov. 3:5). Through this meditation, we seek to deepen our trust in Jesus, whose eternal mercy is our refuge.

The world often seems like an inhospitable place, filled with uncertainty and strife. Doubts may plague our minds, tempting us to rely on our own understanding rather than on God's providence. It is at these times that our need to trust in Jesus becomes most apparent. When we recite the Divine Mercy Chaplet, we acknowledge that only through His mercy can we find true peace and solace. "The Lord is my shepherd; I shall not want" (Ps. 23:1). This assurance frees us from the bondage of fear and anxiety, allowing us to rest in His divine will.

## Trust in the Person of Jesus Christ

Trusting in Jesus means more than believing in His teachings; it is a personal relationship with Him, recognizing Him as our savior and friend. Jesus, who walked upon this earth, understands our human frailties and limitations. He invites us to approach Him with our burdens and to find rest in His love. "Come unto me, all ye that labor and are heavy laden, and I will give you rest" (Matt. 11:28). His words offer a sanctuary where our spirits can rejuvenate, knowing we are cared for by a Divine Friend who endured all that we endure, yet without sin.

One of the most poignant expressions of trust in Jesus is found in His own words during His darkest hour. On the cross, He uttered, "Father, into thy hands I commend my spirit" (Luke 23:46). This ultimate act of surrender is a model for our trust. No matter the depths of our anguish, we can entrust our spirits into the hands of the same loving Father. Through this divine submission, we enter into a union with Christ, sharing in His suffering but also in His victory.

**Trust in His Divine Mercy**

The Divine Mercy Chaplet repeatedly beckons us to plunge into the depths of Jesus' mercy, regardless of

our sins or past mistakes. His mercy is an ocean —
vast, boundless, and inexhaustible. "For as the heaven
is high above the earth, so great is his mercy toward
them that fear him" (Ps. 103:11). This merciful love
invites repentance and conversion, reassuring us that
no sin is too great to be forgiven. When we approach
Jesus with a contrite heart, we experience the
transformative power of His mercy, which cleanses us
from within and renews our spirit.

Our trust in His mercy is not just a passive acceptance
but an active engagement in our relationship with Him.
By invoking His mercy, we commit to living out that
mercy in our own lives. Our trust in Jesus inspires us
to extend forgiveness, compassion, and love to others,
reflecting His divine mercy in our actions and
interactions. This living trust creates ripples of grace,
touching the lives of those around us and drawing them
closer to the heart of God.

**Trust in Times of Suffering**

Suffering is an inevitable part of the human condition,
and it is during these times that our trust in Jesus is
most tested. Yet, it is also in suffering that we find the
greatest opportunity to deepen our trust. Jesus Himself

did not shy away from suffering; instead, He embraced it fully, transforming it into a pathway to redemption. "But he was wounded for our transgressions, he was bruised for our iniquities: the chastisement of our peace was upon him; and with his stripes we are healed" (Isa. 53:5). Through His wounds, we find healing, and through His suffering, we find strength.

In the moments when pain and despair threaten to overwhelm us, trusting in Jesus gives us the courage to persevere. His presence is a balm for our weary souls, and His promises are a beacon of hope. "Yea, though I walk through the valley of the shadow of death, I will fear no evil: for thou art with me; thy rod and thy staff they comfort me" (Ps. 23:4). Knowing that Jesus walks with us in our darkest valleys reassures us that we are never alone. His divine companionship transforms our suffering into an intimate journey with Him, where every sorrow is imbued with the promise of resurrection.

**The Role of Prayer in Trusting Jesus**

Prayer is the lifeline that connects us to Jesus, nurturing and sustaining our trust in Him. The simple, yet profound prayers of the Divine Mercy Chaplet draw us into a deeper communion with Jesus. Each repetition of "For the sake of His sorrowful Passion, have mercy on us and on the whole world" is a cry of trust, a declaration of our reliance on His boundless mercy. "Pray without ceasing" (1 Thess. 5:17) becomes not just a command but a lived experience as we integrate this prayer into our daily lives.

Through prayer, we open our hearts to receive Jesus' guidance and grace. It is our conversation with Him, where we lay bare our doubts, fears, and hopes. In the silence of our hearts, He speaks to us, assuring us of His love and leading us on the path of trust. "Be still, and know that I am God" (Ps. 46:10). This stillness in prayer helps us to discern His will and to trust in His timing. We learn to surrender our plans and desires, confident that His plans for us are good and perfect.

**A Community of Trust**

Trusting in Jesus is not a solitary journey; it is a communal experience. As members of the Body of Christ, we support one another in faith, encouraging and uplifting each other in our walk with the Lord. The community of believers becomes a visible sign of Jesus' presence, a source of strength and hope. "For where two or three are gathered together in my name, there am I in the midst of them" (Matt. 18:20). Together, we build a fortress of trust, embodying the spirit of the Divine Mercy Chaplet in our collective lives.

Our trust in Jesus is expressed in our acts of service and love within the community. By caring for the sick, comforting the sorrowful, and reaching out to the marginalized, we live out the mercy we have received. This active trust transforms our communities, making them places of compassion and grace. It also evangelizes those who witness our lives, drawing them closer to the heart of Jesus

## Contemplations on the Hour of Mercy

At the heart of the Divine Mercy devotion lies the profound significance of the Hour of Mercy. This hour, observed daily at 3 o'clock in the afternoon, marks the moment of our Lord's crucifixion. It is a sacred time for reflection and prayer, commemorating the ultimate act of love and sacrifice that Jesus offered on the cross. "And it was about the sixth hour, and there was a darkness over all the earth until the ninth hour. And the sun was darkened, and the veil of the temple was rent in the midst" (Luke 23:44-45).

This specific hour invites all believers to pause and immerse themselves in the boundless ocean of mercy that flows from Jesus' heart. In this moment, we are called to unite our own sufferings, struggles, and petitions with those of Christ. The Hour of Mercy is not merely a historical remembrance but a living and breathing opportunity to engage with the divine mercy that perpetually seeks to pour out upon the world.

Christ revealed to Saint Faustina that this hour holds exceptional grace and favor. He instructed her to meditate on His Passion and implore His mercy on the world, particularly for sinners. Jesus said, "At three o'clock, implore my mercy, especially for sinners; and, if only for a brief moment, immerse yourself in my Passion, particularly in my abandonment at the moment of agony. This is the hour of great mercy for the whole world" (Diary of Saint Faustina, 1320). These requests underscore the urgency and the power held within these sacred sixty minutes.

The Hour of Mercy is a poignant moment for Knights of Columbus, Patriots, Veterans, Priests, Theologians, and Philosophers alike, to ponder the weight of personal sacrifice. It is an invitation to reflect upon our own contributions towards the greater good and our solidarity with those who suffer. As Christ gave His life without hesitation, we are called to serve selflessly in our vocations and defend the values we hold dear. This hour emboldens us to act courageously, inspired by the ultimate act of valor displayed on Calvary.

Understanding the significance of the Hour of Mercy can transform our daily lives. As we incorporate this observance, we create a sacred rhythm within our routines. Setting aside time at 3 PM, no matter where we are or what we're doing, connects us to Christ's sacrifice and grounds us deeply in His infinite mercy. This simple yet profound practice can foster a moment of stillness and prayer, redirecting our minds and hearts to God, especially amid the busyness of our daily affairs.

For priests and theologians, the Hour of Mercy provides an excellent opportunity to offer their pastoral duties and theological endeavors to Christ. Whether you are in the midst of administering the sacraments, engaging in theological discourse, or writing homilies, this hour asks you to infuse your work with divine mercy, ensuring that it reaches and heals the hearts of those you serve. It is a time to solicit the Lord's strength in your mission and to trust in the transformative power of His Passion.

Similarly, for Veterans and Patriots, the Hour of Mercy can offer a moment of reflection on the sacrifices made for freedom and justice. As you remember the sacrifices of Christ, consider the sacrifices in your own lives and those of your comrades. Absorb the suffering and victory of the Cross as a guiding light for dealing with your wounds, both seen and unseen. It allows for an intimate communion with the Suffering Servant, whose wounds are channels of healing and resurrection.

In varied historical and theological traditions, the Hour of Mercy can also be a time of intense meditation on the nature and presence of divine justice and mercy. Philosophers and contemplative souls may find this hour rich in significance, offering a window to ponder the mysteries of suffering, redemption, and the interplay between divine justice and mercy. This hour becomes a living dialogue with the divine, challenging the mind and heart to delve deeper into divine truths.

The biblical witness reaffirms the profound impact of Jesus' Passion. As Psalm 22 poignantly expresses, "My God, my God, why hast thou forsaken me? Why art thou so far from helping me, and from the words of my roaring?" (Psa. 22:1). The raw emotions of abandonment and despair give way to hope and trust in God's deliverance, mirroring our journey through trials toward ultimate redemption. The Hour of Mercy encapsulates this journey, reminding us that, even in our darkest moments, God's mercy prevails.

For many, the practice of the Divine Mercy Chaplet during this hour enriches the experience. This prayer draws from the depth of Christ's mercy, urging us to repeat with faith, "For the sake of His sorrowful Passion, have mercy on us and on the whole world."

Through this invocation, we not only seek personal mercy but also extend our intercession to the collective needs of humanity. This Chaplet serves as a powerful conduit of grace, binding our intentions with Christ's redemptive act.

Incorporating the Hour of Mercy into the daily rhythm of our lives can foster a transformative shift in our spiritual journey. Allow this hour to become a sanctuary of prayer where your heart finds refuge in the merciful heart of Jesus. Let every heartbeat echo the boundless love that emanates from the cross. As you meditate upon His Passion, envision His wounds becoming sources of healing and channels of grace for your life and the lives of others.

Ultimately, the Hour of Mercy is not just a solitary practice but a communal lifeline. It invites the Church as the Mystical Body of Christ to collectively enter into the vast treasury of God's mercy. As we unite in prayer at this sacred hour, we become instruments of His divine love, cascading mercy upon a world in desperate need of compassion and forgiveness. We stand in solidarity with all the saints and angels, in a choir of intercession, lifting our hearts to the Merciful Savior.

In conclusion, the Hour of Mercy is a profound invitation from Christ to immerse ourselves in His Passion and to trust fully in His inexhaustible mercy. It is a time to align our sufferings with His, to seek His grace, and to intercede for the salvation of the world. As we honor this hour, let us be inspired by the courage, love, and sacrifice of Jesus, allowing His mercy to permeate our lives and flow through us to others. May this contemplation deepen our faith, enliven our spiritual journey, and draw us ever closer to the heart of our Merciful Savior.

## Conclusion

As we navigate the rich tapestry of the Rosary, we uncover the profound mysteries that illuminate our faith and fortify our spirits. Each meditation serves as a cornerstone, reinforcing our understanding of Christ's life and the pivotal role of the Blessed Virgin Mary. Together, we have journeyed through the Joyful, Luminous, Sorrowful, and Glorious Mysteries, as well as the Franciscan Crown Rosary and the Seven Sorrows Servite Rosary. Such reflections cultivate a deeper sense of devotion, guiding us towards the ultimate truth of our faith.

In contemplating these sacred Mysteries, we are reminded of the timeless wisdom found within the Holy Scripture. As it is written, "For where two or three are gathered together in my name, there am I in the midst of them" (Matt. 18:20). Gathering in collective prayer, our faith is both a sanctuary and a fortress, fortified by the words of Christ and the teachings of the Church.

Reflecting on the life of Jesus through the Rosary, we gain insight not only into His divine nature but also His humanity. Each mystery unveils the magnitude of His love and sacrifice. His Baptism, Transfiguration, and ultimate sacrifice on the Cross reveal the profound humility and unwavering obedience to the Father. These reflections are not merely historical recollections but living truths that inspire and transform us, calling us to emulate Christ's humility and love in our daily lives.

Our Blessed Mother's pivotal role in salvation history cannot be understated. "Behold, I am the handmaid of the Lord; be it unto me according to thy word" (Luke 1:38). Mary's fiat echoes through the ages, an eternal testament to faith, obedience, and maternal intercession. Her joys and sorrows become our own as we meditate on the Rosary, deepening our connection to her Immaculate Heart. By venerating Mary, we more closely follow her path to Jesus, her Son and our Redeemer.

Therefore, our commitment to the Rosary is a martial one, for we are called to be spiritual soldiers in a temporal world. Patriotic fervor intertwined with Catholic fervency propels us to defend and uphold the principles upon which our faith stands. As Knights of Columbus, we uphold this honor, courageously defending the truth and serving the less fortunate, embodying the virtues presented to us in the Gospel.

For veterans and patriots, the meditative practice of the Rosary can be a sanctuary of peace. The trials and tribulations of military life find a parallel in the sorrows and sufferings of Jesus and Mary. The Crucifixion echoes the sacrifices made by countless men and women in uniform. Yet, just as Christ rose, so too can they find solace and resurrection in their spiritual lives. "Greater love hath no man than this, that a man lay down his life for his friends" (John 15:13), and in this greatest love, we see reflections of both divine and patriotic sacrifice.

Our dear theologians and philosophers, you delve into the depths of divine mysteries and secular reasoning. The Rosary offers a contemplative lens to marry these pursuits, enabling a balanced approach to understanding God's plan. Through meditative prayer, you tap into a wellspring of divine wisdom, which can illuminate your scholarly endeavors. Philosophical inquiry meets theological certainty in the Marian prayers, creating a robust framework for both faith and reason.

Priests and religious, your leadership within the Church is a beacon of hope for the faithful. Your dedication to Christ, mirrored in daily recitation and living the mysteries of the Rosary, forms the bedrock of ecclesiastical life. By mirroring the attributes of our Blessed Mother and her divine Son, you shepherd the flock towards sanctity. "Let your light so shine before men, that they may see your good works, and glorify your Father which is in heaven" (Matt. 5:16). Your lives are a testament to this divine imperative.

As we close this devotional meditation, let us remember that the journey does not end here. It is but a stepping stone towards deeper faith and more intimate union with God. Convert nonbelievers not merely by words, but through the living testimony of a life transformed by the mysteries of the Rosary. Inspire patriotism by aligning national service with divine service, upholding truth, justice, and the sanctity of human life.

In conclusion, may this book serve as a beacon of faith, a source of inspiration, and a guide for daily living. Let us bind ourselves in unity to praise God, learn from His Word, and emulate the virtues of Christ and Mary. As it is written, "And now abideth faith, hope, charity, these three; but the greatest of these is charity" (1 Cor. 13:13). Let charity guide our actions, faith elevate our spirits, and hope sustain us as we journey ever closer to the eternal embrace of our Heavenly Father.

**Appendix A: Appendix**

As we draw to a close this meditative journey through the Mysteries of our faith, it is fitting to provide an appendix that offers additional spiritual nourishment. This section contains selected **Prayers of the Saints**, inspiring **Quotes from the Saints**, and useful **Historical Notes on the Knights of Columbus**. Each element in this appendix complements the devotional and educational purpose of this book, aiming to deepen your spiritual life and understanding.

**Prayers of the Saints**

The prayers of the saints are timeless treasures that bring us closer to God. They echo through the centuries, reminding us of the saints' unwavering faith. Here are some selected prayers:

- **Prayer of St. Francis of Assisi:** "Lord, make me an instrument of thy peace. Where there is hatred, let me sow love; where there is injury, pardon; where there is doubt, faith; where there is despair, hope; where there is darkness, light; and where there is sadness, joy."

- **Prayer of St. Augustine:** "Breathe in me, O Holy Spirit, that my thoughts may all be holy. Act in me, O Holy Spirit, that my work, too, may be holy. Draw my heart, O Holy Spirit, that I love but what is holy. Strengthen me, O Holy Spirit, to defend all that is holy. Guard me, then, O Holy Spirit, that I always may be holy."

- **Prayer of St. Teresa of Avila:** "Let nothing disturb you, let nothing frighten you, all things are passing; God only is changeless. Patience gains all things. Who has God wants nothing. God alone suffices."

## Quotes from the Saints

The words of the saints offer guidance, wisdom, and encouragement. Here are a few profound quotes for your reflection:

- **St. John Paul II:** "Do not be afraid. Open wide the doors to Christ!"

- **St. Thérèse of Lisieux:** "The world's thy ship, not thy home."

- **St. Thomas Aquinas:** "To one who has faith, no explanation is necessary. To one without faith, no explanation is possible."

- **St. Ignatius of Loyola:** "Go forth and set the world on fire."

- **St. Catherine of Siena:** "Be who God meant you to be and you will set the world on fire."

## Historical Notes on the Knights of Columbus

The Knights of Columbus have played a pivotal role in propagating the Catholic faith and principles of charity, unity, and patriotism since their foundation in 1882 by Father Michael McGivney. Here are some key historical notes:

- **Foundation:** Established to provide financial aid to families with a deceased breadwinner, their mission has grown to include charitable activities, promotion of Catholic education, and defense of religious freedom.

- **Expansion:** From a small group in New Haven, Connecticut, the Knights have expanded to include almost 2 million members worldwide, engaging in numerous charitable endeavors.

- **Patriotism:** Fourth Degree Knights are particularly notable for their patriotic services, including providing honor guards for religious and civic functions, and promoting a better understanding of citizenship responsibilities.

Through the intercession of the saints and the example of the Knights of Columbus, may your journey of faith be enlightened and inspired. As it is written, "I can do all things through Christ which strengtheneth me" (Phil. 4:13).

## Prayers of the Saints

The prayers of the saints have long been the lifeblood of the Church, offering a spiritual bond between the faithful and those who have attained heavenly glory. Saints, in their sanctity and proximity to God, serve as celestial intercessors, ever willing to present our petitions before the Almighty. Their prayers are imbued with a profound love for humanity and a burning desire to see God's will fulfilled on earth as it is in heaven.

In the book of Revelation, we are given a glimpse into the heavenly liturgy where the saints offer our prayers like incense before the throne of God: "And another angel came and stood at the altar, having a golden censer; and there was given unto him much incense, that he should offer it with the prayers of all saints upon the golden altar which was before the throne" (Rev. 8:3). This image not only comforts but also assures us that our prayers are heard and cherished in heaven.

Saint Therese of Lisieux, known as the "Little Flower," is a prime example of a saint whose simplicity and deep trust in God resonate through her prayers. Her "Act of Oblation to Merciful Love" captures her childlike confidence in God's infinite mercy and her desire to become love itself: "O my God! I offer myself as a victim of holocaust to Thy merciful love..." These words echo the sentiment of Psalm 51:17, "The sacrifices of God are a broken spirit: a broken and a contrite heart, O God, thou wilt not despise."

Another luminous figure, Saint Francis of Assisi, offered prayers that continue to inspire with their profound humility and deep connection to creation. His "Canticle of the Sun" invites all creatures to praise the Lord, reflecting a harmonious relationship with all that God has made: "Praised be you, my Lord, with all your creatures, especially Sir Brother Sun..." Saint Francis's prayers remind us of our role as stewards of God's creation and our call to live in harmony with the world around us.

Moreover, the prayers of Saint Augustine reveal a heart deeply yearning for God, capturing the essence of his spiritual journey in his famous prayer: "Thou hast made us for thyself, O Lord, and our heart is restless until it finds its rest in thee." This profound acknowledgment of our innate longing for God echoes the words of Jesus in Matthew 11:28, "Come unto me, all ye that labour and are heavy laden, and I will give you rest."

In times of despair, the prayers of the saints provide a wellspring of hope and courage. Consider the prayer of Saint John of the Cross, whose mystical poetry reflects his deep encounters with divine love even amid the "dark night" of the soul. His prayer, "One dark night, fired with love's urgent longings...," expresses a transcendent trust in God's love, resonant with Psalm 23:4, "Yea, though I walk through the valley of the shadow of death, I will fear no evil: for thou art with me."

The "Hail Mary," inspired by Saint Gabriel's greeting to the Virgin Mary and Elizabeth's exclamation of joy, encapsulates the simplicity and beauty of seeking the intercession of the Queen of All Saints. This prayer, deeply rooted in scripture, invites every believer to find solace and strength under Mary's maternal gaze: "Hail, Mary, full of grace, the Lord is with thee: blessed art thou among women, and blessed is the fruit of thy womb, Jesus" (Luke 1:28, 42). As the Mother of God, her prayers carry a unique potency, reflecting her unparalleled closeness to Jesus.

In the heroic life of Saint Mother Teresa of Calcutta, we see prayers that embody a radical love for the poorest of the poor. Her "Daily Prayer" begins with the poignant request, "Dear Jesus, help me to spread Thy fragrance everywhere I go..." This reflection of her life's work to be Christ's hands and feet in the world mirrors Philippians 1:21, "For to me to live is Christ, and to die is gain."

The prayers of the saints also include those who faced martyrdom with unwavering faith. Saint Thomas More's "Prayer for Good Humor" reveals a man of profound devotion who, even in the face of death, retains a joyful spirit: "Grant me, O Lord, good digestion, and also something to digest..." His calm and joyful acceptance of God's will resonates with James 1:2, "My brethren, count it all joy when ye fall into divers temptations."

Saint Padre Pio, renowned for his stigmata and miraculous intercessions, offered prayers that reflected his profound faith and trust in divine providence. His "Stay with Me, Lord" prayer, recited after Holy Communion, beautifully expresses a deep yearning for Christ's presence: "Stay with me, Lord, for it is necessary to have You present so that I do not forget You..." This aligns with Psalm 27:4, "One thing have I desired of the Lord, that will I seek after; that I may dwell in the house of the Lord all the days of my life, to behold the beauty of the Lord, and to inquire in his temple."

The prayers of the saints offer us a treasure trove of spiritual wisdom, guiding us closer to God while providing intercession and support. They remind us of our connectedness to the Communion of Saints, a spiritual family bound together in Christ's love. As we navigate our earthly pilgrimage, may we draw inspiration from their examples, and through their prayers, find encouragement to remain steadfast in faith, hope, and love. In the timeless words of 1 Thessalonians 5:17, "Pray without ceasing," we are invited to make the prayers of the saints our own, echoing their trust and devotion in every aspect of our lives.

## Quotes from the Saints

The saints, luminous beacons of faith, offer us profound insights and guidance through their words. Their quotes transcend time, providing spiritual nourishment to those who seek enlightenment and solace. As we delve into their testimonies, we are reminded of their unwavering devotion to God and the paths they carved out for us to follow.

"Do not abandon yourselves to despair. We are the Easter people and hallelujah is our song," declared Saint John Paul II. This quote encapsulates the essence of Christian hope and resilience. It assures us that even in moments of darkness, the joy of Christ's resurrection remains our guiding light. This sentiment echoes the words of the Apostle Paul in Romans 12:12, "Rejoicing in hope; patient in tribulation; continuing instant in prayer" (Rom. 12:12).

Saint Teresa of Calcutta, known for her boundless compassion, once said, "Not all of us can do great things. But we can do small things with great love." Her life's work among the poorest of the poor in Calcutta stands testament to this belief. She teaches us that it's not the magnitude of our actions that matters, but the love with which we carry them out. Referencing the Gospel, we find synchrony in the words of Jesus, "And whosoever shall give to drink unto one of these little ones a cup of cold water only in the name of a disciple, verily I say unto you, he shall in no wise lose his reward" (Matt. 10:42).

The mystic Saint John of the Cross offers a vision of the transformative power of divine love. In his poetic language, he reveals, "In the evening of life, we will be judged on love alone." This profound statement draws us to reflect on the ultimate measure of our lives. The Apostle John echoes this in his epistle, "He that loveth not knoweth not God; for God is love" (1 John 4:8).

A contemporary of profound faith, Saint Padre Pio, provides comfort through his assurance, "Pray, hope, and don't worry. Worry is useless. God is merciful and will hear your prayer." Padre Pio's life, marked by miracles and deep spirituality, reminds us of the efficacy of sincere prayer. His emphasis on trust finds resonance in Philippians 4:6, "Be careful for nothing; but in every thing by prayer and supplication with thanksgiving let your requests be made known unto God" (Phil. 4:6).

Moreover, Saint Augustine, one of the Church's greatest theologians, brings forth a philosophical and introspective wisdom: "You have made us for yourself, O Lord, and our hearts are restless until they rest in you." This quote deeply explores the intrinsic longing of the human soul for divine union. It aligns perfectly with the Psalmist's words, "As the hart panteth after the water brooks, so panteth my soul after thee, O God" (Psalm 42:1).

Another theological giant, Saint Thomas Aquinas, declared, "To one who has faith, no explanation is necessary. To one without faith, no explanation is possible." This insight speaks to the profound mystery of faith, which transcends mere reason and logic. It relates to the instruction found in Hebrews 11:1, "Now faith is the substance of things hoped for, the evidence of things not seen" (Heb. 11:1).

Saint Catherine of Siena passionately exhorted, "Be who God meant you to be and you will set the world on fire." Known for her fierce determination and mystical experiences, Catherine encourages us to pursue our God-given purpose with fervor. Jeremiah 29:11 echoes this empowering call, "For I know the plans I have for you, saith the LORD, plans to prosper you, and not to harm you, plans to give you hope and a future" (Jer. 29:11).

Moving into the Renaissance, Saint Ignatius of Loyola contributes a military precision and spiritual clarity: "Go forth and set the world on fire." Much like Catherine's call, Ignatius', grounded in his experience as a soldier turned monk, urges us to evangelization with a deep sense of mission and purpose. His Spiritual Exercises provide a roadmap for disciplined and active faith.

Saint Bernard of Clairvaux penned, "What we love we shall grow to resemble." This Cistercian monk, known for his eloquence and mysticism, imparts the transformative power of love, shaping and molding our very beings into the likeness of Christ. "And we all, who with unveiled faces contemplate the Lord's glory, are being transformed into his image with ever-increasing glory..." (2 Cor. 3:18).

Likewise, Saint Francis of Assisi's simplicity and Franciscan joy resonate in his words, "Preach the Gospel at all times. When necessary, use words." His life of poverty and service embodies the Gospel in action, a call reflected in the Epistle of James, "But be ye doers of the word, and not hearers only..." (James 1:22).

Each saint, a unique vessel of God's grace, offers us a different facet of divine wisdom. Saint Therese of Lisieux, the Little Flower, shares, "The loveliest masterpiece of the heart of God is the heart of a mother." This gently reminds us of the sanctity and beauty of maternal love, mirroring God's own tender care. Isaiah captures this beautifully, "As one whom his mother comforteth, so will I comfort you..." (Isa. 66:13).

Saint Benedict of Nursia, the father of Western monasticism, advises us to "Listen with the ear of your heart." Benedict's Rule, emphasizing humility, silence, and obedience, guides us toward a deeper, contemplative walk with God. The wisdom of Proverbs underlines this counsel, "The ear that heareth the reproof of life abideth among the wise" (Prov. 15:31).

We also draw strength from the words of Saint Joan of Arc, a warrior for God: "I am not afraid... I was born to do this." Joan's undying courage and conviction inspire us to face trials with a similar steadfastness and trust in God's providence, echoing Paul's exhortation to Timothy, "For God hath not given us the spirit of fear;

but of power, and of love, and of a sound mind" (2 Tim. 1:7).

Through their words, the saints continue to teach, inspire, and fortify the faithful. These devout men and women shine forth not as distant figures of the past, but as ever-present companions on our spiritual journey. Their wisdom, etched in divine truth, beckons us to a deeper relationship with God, encouraging us to live out our faith authentically and courageously.

As we meditate on these quotes, let them challenge us to emulate the saints' virtues, hone our spiritual resilience, and foster

## Historical Notes on the Knights of Columbus

The Knights of Columbus, established in 1882, stand as a testament to the enduring power of faith in action. They were founded by Father Michael J. McGivney, a parish priest from New Haven, Connecticut, who witnessed firsthand the trials faced by immigrant and working-class families. His vision was to create a fraternal organization that would offer mutual support and financial aid to members and their families. This mission of charity, unity, and fraternity continues to guide the Knights to this day.

Father McGivney's original inspiration for the Knights came from a deep desire to provide for the spiritual and material welfare of Catholic families. At a time when Catholics faced discrimination and financial hardship, he believed the Church could uplift and unify its community by promoting virtue, fostering mutual aid, and providing insurance to widows and orphans. This vision flowed directly from the Gospel's call to love one another and provide for those in need: "Bear ye one another's burdens, and so fulfil the law of Christ" (Gal. 6:2).

The name "Knights of Columbus" was chosen to honor Christopher Columbus, who was seen as a Catholic symbol of courage and discovery in the American context. The founders wished to demonstrate that Catholics could be both faithful followers of Christ and loyal citizens of the United States. By invoking Columbus, the organization sought to lay claim to an American hero while emphasizing the importance of Catholic contributions to the nation's history.

Over the decades, the Knights of Columbus grew rapidly, establishing councils across North America and eventually spreading globally. Their outreach extended far beyond financial support. They became instrumental in community building, educational programs, and charity work. They supported war efforts, provided disaster relief, and funded numerous Catholic schools and churches. This expansive charitable work is rooted in the Biblical call to serve: "For I was hungry, and ye gave me meat: I was thirsty, and ye gave me drink: I was a stranger, and ye took me in" (Matt. 25:35).

One notable contribution of the Knights is their role in the construction of the National Shrine of the Immaculate Conception in Washington, D.C. This national shrine, dedicated to the Blessed Virgin Mary, became a manifestation of the Knights' devotion to Mary and their commitment to the Catholic faith. Its construction was largely supported by the financial and volunteer efforts of the Knights, showcasing their dedication to beautifying places of worship and enhancing the spiritual life of Catholics in the United States.

The Knights also played a vital role in promoting Catholic education. In response to the increasing secularization of public schools, they established scholarships, endowments, and supported Catholic universities. By doing so, they ensured that Catholic values and teachings could continue to be passed down to future generations, preserving the rich tradition of Catholic intellectual thought. The importance of this mission is underscored by Proverbs 22:6: "Train up a child in the way he should go: and when he is old, he will not depart from it."

In addition to their educational initiatives, the Knights of Columbus have been staunch defenders of the sanctity of life. They have supported numerous pro-life organizations and initiatives, advocating for the unborn and providing resources for mothers in need. Their commitment to life from conception to natural death is reflective of the Church's teachings and the belief in the inherent dignity of every human being, as stated in Psalm 139:13-14: "For thou hast possessed my reins: thou hast covered me in my mother's womb. I will praise thee; for I am fearfully and wonderfully made."

The Knights also promote patriotism and civic involvement through their Fourth Degree, known as the Patriotic Degree. Members of this degree pledge to live out the principles of patriotism, defined by love for both God and country. They actively participate in public life, military service, and community events, embodying the spirit of true patriotism that respects and upholds the freedoms enshrined in the Constitution while guided by moral and ethical values grounded in Christian faith.

As part of their mission to uphold the principles of unity and fraternity, the Knights have worked tirelessly to support their fellow members and communities. This fraternity is not just a fellowship of convenience but a divine call to unity, as echoed in Psalm 133:1 – "Behold, how good and how pleasant it is for brethren to dwell together in unity!" This unity has manifested in various ways across different cultures and communities, adapting to the needs of the time while steadfastly holding to the core values of charity, unity, and fraternity.

In modern times, the Knights of Columbus have continued to adapt and respond to contemporary challenges. They have embraced technology to enhance communication and mobilize resources for global charitable initiatives. During the COVID-19 pandemic, they provided essential services, such as food distribution, blood drives, and financial assistance to those affected by the crisis. Their quick and effective response demonstrated their ongoing commitment to living out the corporal works of mercy in real and tangible ways.

Moreover, the Knights have focused on addressing issues of religious liberty. Where the freedom of religious expression is being challenged, they have taken a stand to defend the rights of Catholics and people of all faiths. Their advocacy efforts align with the founding principles of freedom and equality, emphasizing that true freedom is grounded in moral truth and respect for the divine law, as found in 2 Corinthians 3:17: "Now the Lord is that Spirit: and where the Spirit of the Lord is, there is liberty."

One continuously growing initiative of the Knights is their men's spiritual formation programs. Recognizing the crucial role of men as spiritual leaders within their families and communities, the Knights have developed resources and programs to strengthen their faith and commitment. These programs often include prayer groups, Bible studies, and retreats, fostering a deeper understanding of their vocation and mission as Catholic men. This focus on spiritual growth is reminiscent of Saint Paul's exhortation in 1 Timothy 6:11-12: "But thou, O man of God, flee these things; and follow after righteousness, godliness, faith, love, patience, meekness. Fight the good fight of faith, lay hold on eternal life."

In summary, the history of the Knights of Columbus is rich with examples of faith in action, a testament to the enduring power of charity, unity, and fraternity in the Catholic tradition. From their humble beginnings in New Haven to their expansive global presence today, the Knights have consistently upheld the values and teachings of the Church through various charitable, educational, and patriotic endeavors. Their story is one of resilience, dedication, and unwavering commitment to the principles of Christian brotherhood and public service, inspired by the Gospel's call to love and serve God and neighbor alike.


## THE 15 PRAYERS OF ST. BRIDGET

These Prayers and these Promises have been copied from a book printed in Toulouse in 1740 and published by the P. Adrien Parvilliers of the Company of Jesus, Apostolic Missionary of the Holy Land, with approbation, permission and recommendation to distribute them.

Pope Pius IX took cognisance of these Prayers with the prologue; he approved them May 31, 1862, recognising them as true and for the good of souls.


As St. Bridget for a long time wanted to know the number of blows Our Lord received during His Passion, He one day appeared to her and said: "I received 5480 blows on My Body. If you wish to honour them in some way, say 15 Our Fathers and 15 Hail Marys with the following Prayers (which He taught her) for a whole year. When the year is up, you will have honoured each one of My Wounds."

**He made the following promises to anyone who recited these Prayers for a whole year:**

1. I will deliver 15 souls of his lineage from Purgatory.

2. 15 souls of his lineage will be confirmed and preserved in grace.

3. 15 sinners of his lineage will be converted.

4. Whoever recites these Prayers will attain the first degree of perfection.

5. 15 days before his death I will give him My Precious Body in order that he may escape eternal starvation; I will give him My Precious Blood to drink lest he thirst eternally.

6. 15 days before his death he will feel a deep contrition for all his sins and will have a perfect knowledge of them.

7. I will place before him the sign of My Victorious Cross for his help and defence against the attacks of his enemies.

8. Before his death I shall come with My Dearest Beloved Mother.

9. I shall graciously receive his soul, and will lead it into eternal joys.

10. And having led it there I shall give him a special draught from the fountain of My Deity, something I will not for those who have not recited My Prayers.

11. Let it be known that whoever may have been living in a state of mortal sin for 30 years, but who will recite devoutly, or have the intention to recite these Prayers, the Lord will forgive him all his sins.

12. I shall protect him from strong temptations.

13. I shall preserve and guard his 5 senses.

14. I shall preserve him from a sudden death.

15. His soul will be delivered from eternal death.

16. He will obtain all he asks for from God and the Blessed Virgin.

17. If he has lived all his life doing his own will and he is to die the next day, his life will be prolonged.

18. Every time one recites these Prayers he gains 100 days indulgence.

19. He is assured of being joined to the supreme Choir of Angels.

20. Whoever teaches these Prayers to another, will have continuous joy and merit which will endure eternally.

21. There where these Prayers are being said or will be said in the future God is present with His grace.

**Each prayer is preceded by one Our Father and one Hail Mary.**

**Our Father**, who art in heaven, hallowed be thy name.
Thy kingdom come.
Thy will be done on earth as it is in heaven.
Give us this day our daily bread and forgive us our
trespasses as we forgive those who trespass against us
and lead us not into temptation but deliver us from
evil.  **Amen**

**Hail Mary**, full of grace, the Lord is with thee; blessed
art thou among women and blessed is the fruit of thy
womb, Jesus.
Holy Mary, Mother of God, pray for us sinners, now and
at the hour of our death.  **Amen.**

**FIRST PRAYER**

**Our Father – Hail Mary.**

O Jesus Christ! Eternal Sweetness to those who love Thee, joy surpassing all joy and all desire, Salvation and Hope of all sinners, Who hast proved that Thou hast no greater desire than to be among men, even assuming human nature at the fullness of time for the love of men, recall all the sufferings Thou hast endured from the instant of Thy conception, and especially during Thy Passion, as it was decreed and ordained from all eternity in the Divine plan.

Remember, O Lord, that during the Last Supper with Thy disciples, having washed their feet, Thou gavest them Thy Most Precious Body and Blood, and while at the same time thou didst sweetly console them, Thou didst foretell them Thy coming Passion.
Remember the sadness and bitterness which Thou didst experience in Thy Soul as Thou Thyself bore witness saying: "My Soul is sorrowful even unto death."

Remember all the fear, anguish and pain that Thou didst suffer in Thy delicate Body before the torment of the Crucifixion, when, after having prayed three times, bathed in a sweat of blood, Thou wast betrayed by Judas, Thy disciple, arrested by the people of a nation

Thou hadst chosen and elevated, accused by false witnesses, unjustly judged by three judges during the flower of Thy youth and during the solemn Paschal season.

Remember that Thou wast despoiled of Thy garments and clothed in those of derision; that Thy Face and Eyes were veiled, that Thou wast buffeted, crowned with thorns, a reed placed in Thy Hands, that Thou was crushed with blows and overwhelmed with affronts and outrages.

In memory of all these pains and sufferings which Thou didst endure before Thy Passion on the Cross, grant me before my death true contrition, a sincere and entire confession, worthy satisfaction and the remission of all my sins. **Amen.**

**SECOND PRAYER**

**Our Father – Hail Mary.**

O Jesus! True liberty of angels, Paradise of delights, remember the horror and sadness which Thou didst endure when Thy enemies, like furious lions, surrounded Thee, and by thousands of insults, spits, blows, lacerations and other unheard-of-cruelties, tormented Thee at will.

In consideration of these torments and insulting words, I beseech Thee, O my Saviour, to deliver me from all my enemies, visible and invisible, and to bring me, under Thy protection, to the perfection of eternal salvation. **Amen.**

**THIRD PRAYER**

**Our Father – Hail Mary.**

O Jesus! Creator of Heaven and earth Whom nothing can encompass or limit, Thou Who dost enfold and hold all under Thy Loving power, remember the very bitter pain.

Thou didst suffer when the Jews nailed Thy Sacred Hands and Feet to the Cross by blow after blow with big blunt nails, and not finding Thee in a pitiable enough state to satisfy their rage, they enlarged Thy Wounds, and added pain to pain, and with indescribable cruelty stretched Thy Body on the Cross, pulled Thee from all sides, thus dislocating Thy Limbs.

I beg of Thee, O Jesus, by the memory of this most Loving suffering of the Cross, to grant me the grace to fear Thee and to Love Thee. **Amen.**

## FOURTH PRAYER

**Our Father – Hail Mary.**

O Jesus! Heavenly Physician, raised aloft on the Cross to heal our wounds with Thine, remember the bruises which Thou didst suffer and the weakness of all Thy Members which were distended to such a degree that never was there pain like unto Thine.

From the crown of Thy Head to the Soles of Thy Feet there was not one spot on Thy Body that was not in torment, and yet, forgetting all Thy sufferings, Thou didst not cease to pray to Thy Heavenly Father for Thy enemies, saying: "Father forgive them for they know not what they do."

Through this great Mercy, and in memory of this suffering, grant that the remembrance of Thy Most Bitter Passion may effect in us a perfect contrition and the remission of all our sins. **Amen**.

**FIFTH PRAYER**

**Our Father – Hail Mary.**

O Jesus! Mirror of eternal splendour, remember the sadness which Thou experienced, when contemplating in the light of Thy Divinity the predestination of those who would be saved by the merits of Thy Sacred Passion.

Thou didst see at the same time, the great multitude of reprobates who would be damned for their sins, and Thou didst complain bitterly of those hopeless lost and unfortunate sinners.

Through this abyss of compassion and pity, and especially through the goodness which Thou displayed to the good thief when Thou saidst to him: "This day, thou shalt be with Me in Paradise." I beg of Thee, O Sweet Jesus, that at the hour of my death, Thou wilt show me mercy. **Amen**.

**SIXTH PRAYER**

**Our Father – Hail Mary.**

O Jesus! Beloved and most desirable King, remember

the grief Thou didst suffer, when naked and like a common criminal.

Thou was fastened and raised on the Cross, when all Thy relatives and friends abandoned Thee, except Thy Beloved Mother, who remained close to Thee during Thy agony and whom Thou didst entrust to Thy faithful disciple when Thou saidst to Mary: "Woman, behold thy son!" and to St. John: "Son, behold thy Mother!"

I beg of Thee O my Saviour, by the sword of sorrow which pierced the soul of Thy holy Mother, to have compassion on me in all my affliction and tribulations, both corporal and spiritual, and to assist me in all my trials, and especially at the hour of my death. **Amen**.

**SEVENTH PRAYER**

**Our Father – Hail Mary.**

O Jesus! Inexhaustible Fountain of compassion, Who by a profound gesture of Love, said from the Cross: "I thirst!" suffered from the thirst for the salvation of the human race.

I beg of Thee O my Saviour, to inflame in our hearts the

desire to tend toward perfection in all our acts; and to extinguish in us the concupiscence of the flesh and the ardor of worldly desires. **Amen**.

## EIGHTH PRAYER

**Our Father – Hail Mary.**

O Jesus! Sweetness of hearts, delight of the spirit, by the bitterness of the vinegar and gall which Thou didst taste on the Cross for Love of us, grant us the grace to receive worthily.

Thy Precious Body and Blood during our life and at the hour of our death, that they may serve as a remedy and consolation for our souls. **Amen.**

## NINTH PRAYER

**Our Father – Hail Mary.**

O Jesus! Royal virtue, joy of the mind, recall the pain Thou didst endure when, plunged in an ocean of bitterness at the approach of death, insulted, outraged by the Jews.

Thou didst cry out in a loud voice that Thou was

abandoned by Thy Father, saying: "My God, My God, why hast Thou forsaken me?"

Through this anguish, I beg of Thee, O my Saviour, not to abandon me in the terrors and pains of my death. **Amen.**

**TENTH PRAYER**

**Our Father – Hail Mary.**

O Jesus! Who art the beginning and end of all things, life and virtue, remembers that for our sakes Thou was plunged in an abyss of suffering from the soles of Thy Feet to the crown of Thy Head.

In consideration of the enormity of Thy Wounds, teach me to keep, through pure love, Thy Commandments, whose way is wide and easy for those who love Thee. **Amen.**

**ELEVENTH PRAYER**

**Our Father – Hail Mary.**

O Jesus! Deep abyss of mercy, I beg of Thee, in memory of Thy Wounds which penetrated to the very marrow of

Thy Bones and to the depth of Thy being, to draw me, a miserable sinner, overwhelmed by my offenses, away from sin and to hide me from Thy Face justly irritated against me, hide me in Thy wounds, until Thy anger and just indignation shall have passed away. **Amen.**

**TWELFTH PRAYER**

**Our Father – Hail Mary.**

O Jesus! Mirror of Truth, symbol of unity, bond of charity, remember the multitude of wounds with which Thou wast afflicted from head to foot, torn and reddened by the spilling of Thy adorable Blood. O great and universal pain, which Thou didst suffer in Thy virginal flesh for love of us! Sweetest Jesus! What is there that Thou couldst have done for us which Thou has not done!

May the fruit of Thy suffering be renewed in my soul by the faithful remembrance of Thy Passion, and may Thy love increase in my heart each day, until I see Thee in eternity: Thou Who art the treasure of every real good and every joy, which I beg Thee to grant me, O Sweetest Jesus, in heaven. **Amen.**

**THIRTEENTH PRAYER**

**Our Father – Hail Mary.**

O Jesus! Strong Lion, Immortal and Invincible King, remember the pain which Thou didst endure when all Thy strength, both moral and physical, was entirely exhausted, Thou didst bow Thy Head, saying: "It is consummated!"

Through this anguish and grief, I beg of Thee Lord Jesus, to have mercy on me at the hour of my death when my mind will be greatly troubled and my soul will be in anguish. **Amen.**

**FOURTEENTH PRAYER**

**Our Father – Hail Mary.**

O Jesus! Only Son of the Father, Splendour and Figure of His Substance, remember the simple and humble recommendation.

Thou didst make of Thy Soul to Thy Eternal Father, saying: "Father, into Thy Hands I commend My Spirit!" And with Thy Body all torn, and Thy Heart Broken, and the bowels of Thy Mercy open to redeem us, Thou didst

Expire.

By this Precious Death, I beg of Thee O King of Saints, comfort me and help me to resist the devil, the flesh and the world, so that being dead to the world I may live for Thee alone.

I beg of Thee at the hour of my death to receive me, a pilgrim and an exile returning to Thee. **Amen.**

**FIFTEENTH PRAYER**

**Our Father – Hail Mary.**

O Jesus! True and fruitful Vine! Remember the abundant outpouring of Blood which Thou didst so generously shed from Thy Sacred Body as juice from grapes in a wine press.

From Thy Side, pierced with a lance by a soldier, blood and water issued forth until there was not left in Thy Body a single drop, and finally, like a bundle of myrrh lifted to the top of the Cross Thy delicate Flesh was destroyed, the very Substance of Thy Body withered, and the Marrow of Thy Bones dried up.

Through this bitter Passion and through the outpouring of Thy Precious Blood, I beg of Thee, O Sweet Jesus, to receive my soul when I am in my death agony.  **Amen.**


**CONCLUSION**

O Sweet Jesus! Pierce my heart so that my tears of penitence and love will be my bread day and night; may I be converted entirely to Thee, may my heart be Thy perpetual habitation, may my conversation be pleasing to Thee, and may the end of my life be so praiseworthy that I may merit Heaven and there with Thy saints, praise Thee forever.  **Amen.**